Detecting High Profit Day Trades In The Futures Markets

Using Zone Pattern Probability Analysis

By J. T. Jackson

Windsor Books, Brightwaters, N.Y.

Published by Windsor Books
P.O. Box 280
Brightwaters, N.Y. 11718

Manufactured in the United States of America

ISBN 0-930233-55-7

INTRODUCTION

Introduction

Zone Pattern Probability Analysis is a method for trading futures based on statistical projections from historical market data. The method was designed initially for a CBOT exchange member to trade US Treasury Bonds on an intraday basis. The concepts and databases developed are applicable, however, to traders of other futures markets and various time frames. For intraday traders, Zone Pattern Probabilities show where prices are likely to trade during the day, where the market should run, and where the market should stop and reverse. For day traders, Zone Pattern Probabilities show a high probability range to place a trade for the day, a strategic location to place a protective stop, and the probability the stop will be hit. For position traders, Zone Pattern Probabilities help to pinpoint market entry or to scale in large positions with increased risk/reward ratios.

This trading approach uses construction of price zones and probability tables from statistical analysis. The analysis offers many advantages for traders. A list of some of these advantages include:

- Applicable to all futures markets

- Adaptable to different time frames and trading styles

- Incorporates the two most important factors affecting daily price movement (based on my research)

- Generates probabilities based on more than ten years of historical testing

- Shows the presence of high probability zones for profitable trades during the day

- Allows the trader to determine the frequency of trading and the advantage over the market

- Can be used in conjunction with other systems and technical indicators

- Can be used without a computer

In this book the background and evolution of Zone Pattern Probability Analysis is introduced. Discussion of the rationale for the concept of price zones and probability tables are presented in nine sections under the titles given on the next page. Illustrative pattern examples in the use of Zone Pattern Probabilities are shown in Section 8 and Section 9. Practical steps in the application of this approach and extensive databases are given in three Appendices.

Sections

Appendices

SECTION 1:

ZONES — A LONG-TERM PERSPECTIVE

The concept of price zones was introduced by the publications of commodity trader, Dr. Bruce Gould. Dr. Gould suggested dividing historical prices into 5 zones in which each zone represents 20% of the price range for the previous three years. For example, graph #1 (on the following page) shows the weekly range of wheat prices for 1988, 1989, and 1990 divided into price zones.

The highest price of wheat during this period was $4.26, and the lowest price was $2.56. The variation of the price range was $1.70 which when divided into 5 zones amounts to a difference of 34 cents each. Zone1 contains the lowest 20% of the previous price range which extends from $2.56 to $2.90. Zone2 contains the next fifth between 20% to 40% of the previous price range which extends from $2.90 to $3.24. Zone3 contains the next fifth between 40% to 60% of the price range extending from $3.24 to $3.58. Zone4 contains the next fifth between 60% to 80% of the previous price range extending from $3.58 to $3.92. And Zone5 represents the final 20% between 80% to 100% of the previous range from $3.92 to $4.26.

Dividing past prices into zones places current prices into the context of market perspective. For example, according to Dr. Gould, if you want to consider aggressive buying in wheat, prices ideally should be in Zone1 or Zone2. If prices are in Zone4 or Zone5, you must accept more risk and reduced likelihood of big gains. At the end of 1990 wheat prices were in Zone1. As illustrated by the subsequent graph of 1991 wheat prices (graph #2), by mid-1991 prices had rallied to nearly $3.50, placing the market price in Zone4. Thus as the strategy of zone-derived risk/reward ratios suggested, the purchase of wheat futures in Zone1 (end of 1990) provided an excellent opportunity for an aggressive long investment.

The concept of price zones works because of the cyclical nature of commodity markets. Commodities like wheat never fail completely nor become so abundant as to destroy the market. Thus the market reflects the constantly changing prices of supply and demand. Establishing historical price zones provides a way of measuring this cyclicality in relation to recent highs and lows. For example, recent wheat prices were in Zone5 which is high compared with recent historical ranges. Just as Zone1 provides a good buying opportunity, so does Zone5 provide a good selling opportunity. When prices have reached Zone5, the price zone strategy can be reversed for short selling by the aggressive trader. As illustrated by graph #3, the results would have been a large gain when selling short in Zone5.

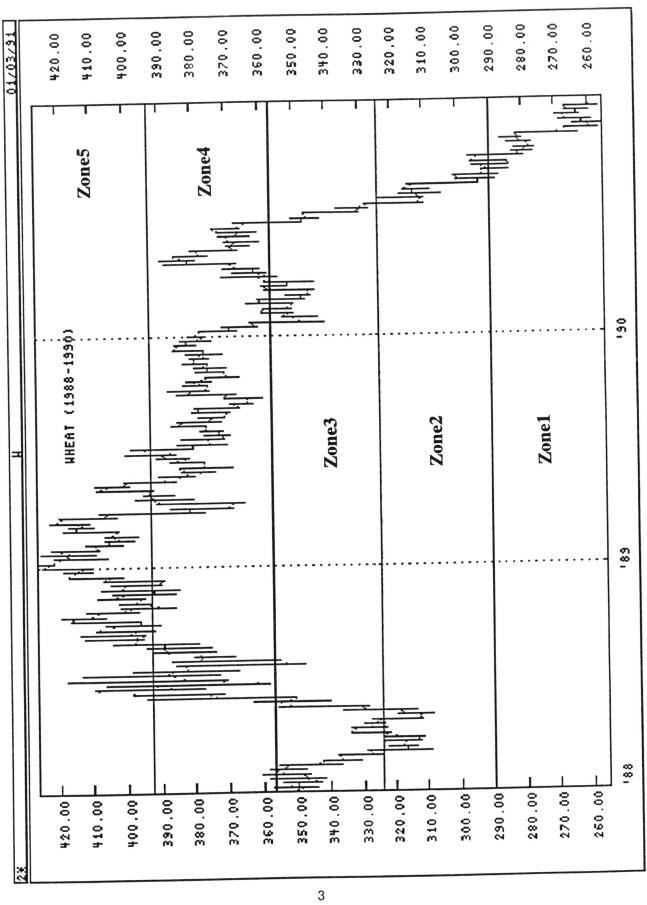

Graph #1

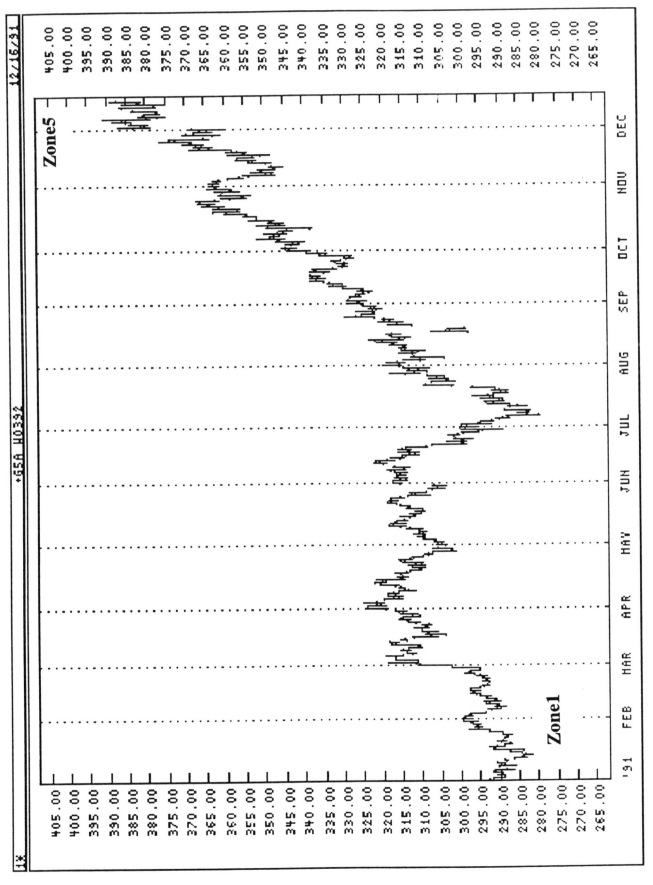

Graph #2

4

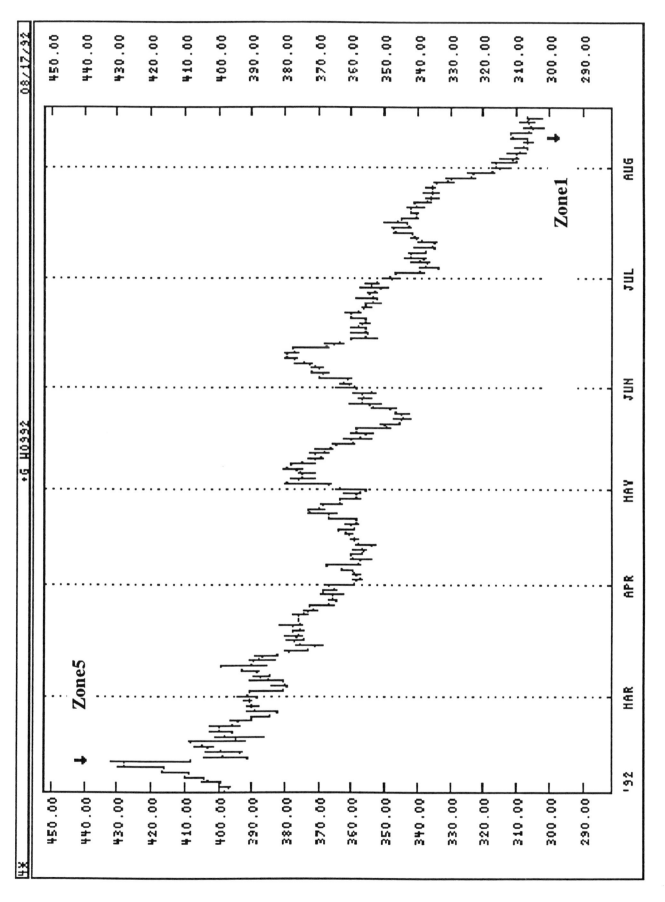

Graph #3

SECTION 2:

ZONES — A SHORT-TERM PERSPECTIVE

Zone analysis, as with most technical indicators, can be applied over different time frames. For traders using short time frames, daily rather than yearly price zones are required. Price zones for each day could be constructed following the principles outlined in Section 1. However, in the development of Zone Pattern Probabilities, it was ascertained that rather than dividing the day into five equal 20% regions (as with long-term zones), it would be more effective if the zone boundaries were placed at strategic daily locations of projected price support and resistance. One well-known formula, still conscientiously followed by floor traders, computes five boundaries of expected support and resistance levels of prices based on the previous day's high, low, and close. The formula for computing the levels is given below:

Daily Zone Formation

———————————— $High2 = Avg + High\ 1 - Low\ 1$ ————————————

———————————— $High1 = (2 * Avg) - Low$ ————————————

———————————— $Avg = (High + Low + Close)\ /3$ ————————————

———————————— $Low1 = (2 * Avg) - High$ ————————————

———————————— $Low2 = Avg + Low1 - High1$ ————————————

Using this formula the five price levels create a total of <u>six</u> zones, i.e., the areas above, below, and between the five price limits, rather than the long-term method which uses only five zones. Zone1 is any price below Low2 and has no lower boundary. Zone2 falls between Low2 and Low1. Zone3 falls between Low1 and the Average (Avg). Zone4 falls between the Average and High1. Zone5 falls between High1 and High2. Zone 6 is any price above High2 and has no upper boundary. For each of these zones, the price action can be character-ized as follows:

Zone Price Action

Zone6 : strongly up

Zone5 : moderately up

Zone4 : mildly up

Zone3 : mildly down

Zone2 : moderately down

Zone1 : strongly down

As noted, this method of determining divisions within recent price support and resistance action in the market is not a unique feature of Zone Pattern Probability Analysis. What is unique to this analysis is utilizing the idea of strategic price zones combined with computing an additional statistical probability for the price support and resistance within the range of price zones. The probabilities discussed in the next section can be used to determine where to place buy and sell orders for strategic entry and exit points.

SECTION 3:

COMBINING ZONES AND PROBABILITY

By establishing price zones derived from the daily market action, historical data can be analyzed to determine the probability of directional changes when the price reaches any particular zone. The probabilities for directional zone action are developed from the answers to three questions:

1) What percentage of days do prices reach a particular zone?
2) If prices reach a lower zone, what percentage of days is that the low zone for the day?
3) If prices reach a higher zone, what percentage of days is that the high zone for the day?

Statistical analysis to obtain an answer to question #1 defines a value designated as Zone Reached. A similar solution to question #2 gives a probability value defined as Zone Support. The solution to question #3 gives the probability value for Zone Resistance. To compute the probabilities for Zone Reached, Zone Support, and Zone Resistance, a software program was developed and futures data were tested over a ten year time span. The examples below use the test results from S&P data.

Zone Reached

On what percentage of days does the S&P reach each particular price zone when six price zones for the S&P are established from the market action of the preceding day (following the scheme given in Section 2)? The probabilities from the test results are as follows:

Zone Number	Zone Reached
6	20%
5	44%
4	83%
3	79%
2	42%
1	20%

Below is a histogram showing the frequency each zone is reached.

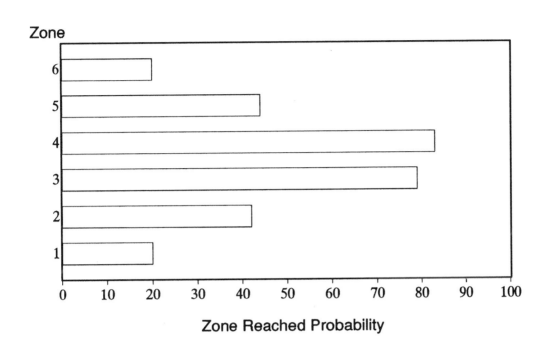

Zone Reached Probability

The results show the market produces a normal frequency (Gautian distribution) curve for the zone reached within the six zone range. The symmetry of the curve shows no inherent market biases affecting the movement of the S&P over the 10 year time span. There is a high level of frequency with which prices moved throughout the price range, i.e., the sum of the Zone Reached probabilities equals 288%. This suggests that on any given day the statistical probability is that the Zone Reached includes two or three of the six price zones.

This data is useful as it reveals the frequency of opportunity for making a trade in a particular zone. The two extreme low and high price zones (Zone1 and Zone6) are reached on approximately 20% of the days. The two intermediate zones (Zone2 and Zone5) are reached on slightly more than 40% of the days. The two central price zones (Zone3 and Zone4) are reached on approximately 80% of the days. This tells us, for example, that if you want to sell an S&P contract in Zone5, historically you'll have a chance to make that trade 44% of the time.

Zone Resistance

When prices reach one of the higher zones, what percentage of the time is that the highest zone for the day, i.e., prices meet resistance? Historically, the S&P has the following percentages:

Zone Number	Zone Reached	Zone Resistance
6	20%	39%
5	44%	54%
4	83%	49%

The histogram below shows the zone resistance percentage graphically with the light grey bars, as well as the zone reached percentage with the white bars.

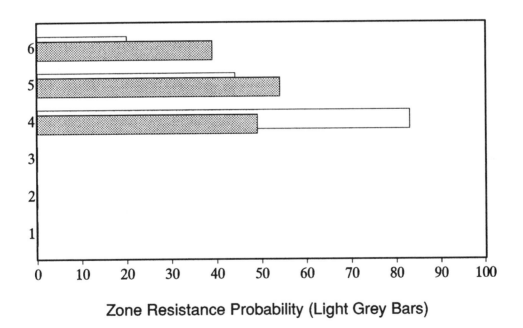

Zone Resistance Probability (Light Grey Bars)

If prices reach Zone4, 49% of the time Zone4 is the high zone. If prices reach Zone5, 54% of the time Zone5 is the high zone. If prices reach Zone6, then by definition Zone6 is the high zone that day since there is no upper boundary. Zone6 resistance is defined as prices breaking to close in a lower zone. For Zone6, 39% of the time prices find resistance and close in a lower zone. Using

these zone probabilities, what trading statistics can be developed for each of these zones?

Zone4 Trades: There is an 83% chance of making the trade. If you sell in Zone4 and place a buy stop in Zone5, there is a 49% chance your stop will not be reached.

Zone5 Trades: There is a 44% chance of making the trade. If you sell in Zone5 and place a buy stop in Zone6, there is a 54% chance your stop will not be reached.

Zone6 Trades: There is a 20% chance of making the trade. If you sell as prices enter Zone6 and hold to the close, there is a 39% chance prices will close below Zone6 for a profitable trade. (If you buy as prices enter Zone6, there is a (100% - 39% =) 61% chance of prices remaining higher for a profitable trade.)

Zone Support

When the Zone Reached is one of the three lower zones, on what percentage of the days is that zone the lowest for the day? Historically, the S&P has the following price action:

Zone Number	Zone Reached	Zone Support
3	79%	49%
2	42%	54%
1	20%	45%

The histogram on the next page shows the zone support percentage graphically with the dark grey bars, as well as the zone reached percentage with the white bars.

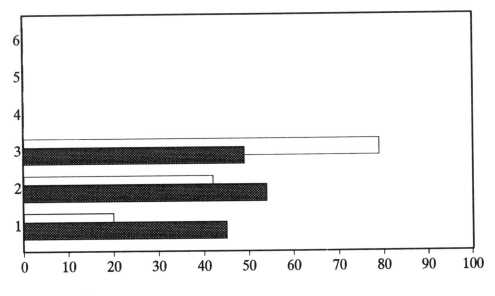

Zone Support Probability (Dark Grey Bars)

If prices reach Zone3, it is the lowest zone on 49% of the days. If prices reach Zone2, 54% of the time Zone 2 is the low zone. If prices reach Zone1, then by definition Zone1 is the low zone since there is no lower boundary. Zone1 support is defined as prices rallying to close in a higher zone. For Zone1, 45% of the time prices find support and reverse to close in a higher zone.

Using the concept of zone probabilities just explained, what trading statistics can be developed for each of these zones?

> Zone3 Trades: There is a 79% chance of making the trade. If you buy in Zone3 and place a sell stop in Zone2, there is a 49% chance your stop will not be reached.
>
> Zone2 Trades: There is a 42% chance of making the trade. If you buy in Zone2 and place a sell stop in Zone1, there is a 54% chance your stop will not be reached.
>
> Zone1 Trades: There is a 20% chance of making the trade. If you buy as prices enter Zone1 and hold to the close, there is a 45% chance prices will close above Zone1 for a profitable trade. (If you sell as prices enter Zone1, there is a (100%-45% =) 55% chance of prices remaining lower for a profitable trade.)

14

In summary, the observed probabilities for Zone Reached are established by prices crossing the border into that zone. On the other hand, the Zone Support and Zone Resistance probabilities are established only when prices enter into the zone, but do not breach the opposite border of the zone.

The combined graph including Zone Reached, Zone Resistance, and Zone Support now appears as follows. The white bars represent the percentage of days each zone is reached, the light grey bars represent the frequency of zone resistance, and the dark grey bars represent the frequency of zone support for that portion of the sample that enters each specific zone.

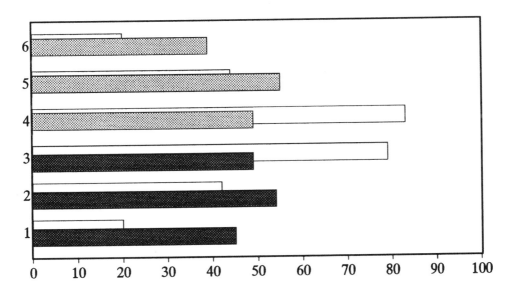

Frequency of Zone Reached and Support / Resistance

SECTION 4:

COMBINING ZONES AND PROBABILITY WITH TECHNICAL ANALYSIS

What is the purpose of plotting the frequency distribution of price action and behavior? The goal is to find daily trading opportunities where the zone support and resistance probabilities are significantly higher or lower than 50%. The previous graphs shown with zone support and resistance probabilities ranging between 45% to 55% won't provide the basis for a desirable trading strategy. To improve these probabilities, a number of technical analysis indicators were tested in conjunction with the zone probabilities. These technical indicators include:

- Zone price above moving average / below moving average

- Zone price overbought / price oversold

- Zone trending market / non-trending market

- Zone higher close / lower close

- Zone higher open / lower open

- Zone increased volume / decreased volume

- Zone close / zone open

- Zone position in cycle measurement

- Zone filled gaps / unfilled gaps

- Zone inside days / outside days

- Zone reversal days / pivot days

- Zone high congestion/low congestion

- Zone highest high/low/close in #n days

- Zone lowest high/low/close in #n days

Moving averages are among the simplest and most well-known technical indicators. If prices are above the moving average, that condition is considered bullish. If prices are below the moving average, that condition is considered bearish. In conjunction with zone probabilities the questions to test are: If prices are above the moving average, is there a large increase in zone support? If prices are below the moving average, is there a large increase in zone resistance? The length of a moving average is a variable parameter. The results shown in the graphs that follow incorporate a 21-day moving average.

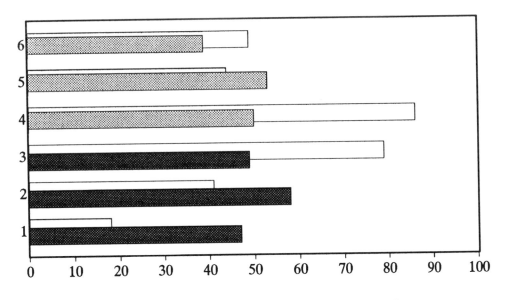

Probability Distribution with Close > 21-Day Average

As seen in the results from the graph above, if the price is greater than the moving average, Zone2 support increases from 54% to 58%. So there is a slight increase in the Zone2 support value when the closing price is above its 21-day moving average. Although this is an improvement, to achieve a profitable trading strategy a higher probability would be desirable.

Consider the graph below when the close was below the 21-day average.

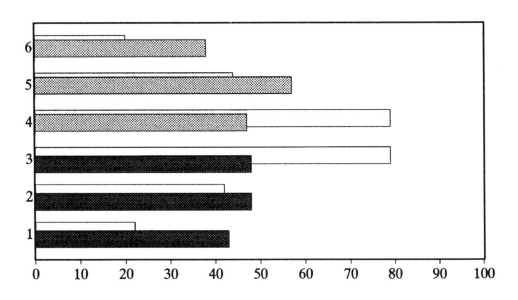

Probability Distribution with Close < 21-Day Average

Results are similar for Zone5 with slightly less support and more resistance when the closing price is below its 21-day moving average. Zone5 resistance increased from 54% to 59%. Again, a higher zone resistance value would be desirable.

Stochastics is another technical indicator which is currently very popular. In theory, when prices are oversold they should tend to provide support; when prices are overbought they should tend to provide resistance. In conjunction with zone probabilities the questions to test are: If prices are oversold, do the zone support probabilities significantly increase? If prices are overbought, do the zone resistance percentages significantly increase? The results are shown in the graphs that follow.

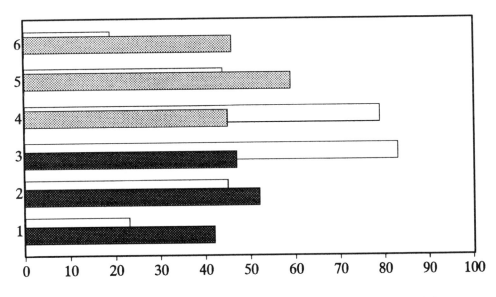

Probability Distribution with 5-Day Stochastic < 20

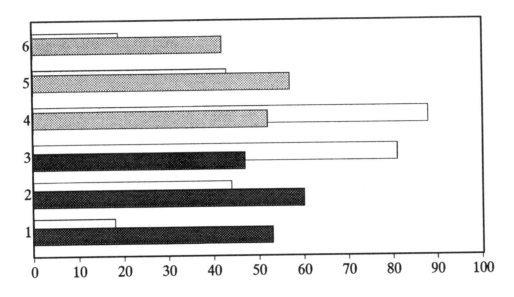

Probability Distribution with 5-Day Stochastic > 80

Notice in the results that when a 5-bar daily stochastic is below 20, Zone2 support actually decreased from 54% to 52% and Zone5 resistance increased from 54% to 61%. When a 5-bar daily stochastic was above 80 the same contrary results occurred. Zone5 resistance increased from 54% to 58% but Zone2 support increased even more, from 54% to 61%. These results suggest that an overbought stochastic may imply further buying and an oversold stochastic may imply further selling. Again, none of these results produce significantly increased probabilities on which to base a trading strategy.

After extensive testing of numerous technical indicators in a similar fashion, the results establish the following conclusions:

1. **Today's opening zone is the most significant factor affecting today's price.**
2. **Yesterday's closing zone is the second most significant factor affecting today's price.**

Using the close and open together, as a combination or pattern, can drastically improve the probabilities. Why does using close/open patterns produce significant probabilities? One answer is that potentially profitable day trades are often created from an inconsistency between yesterday's close and today's open. For example, if prices closed yesterday in Zone6 (strongly up), the

majority of time prices will open today in Zone4 (steady to a little better). If prices now open substantially lower, a potentially profitable trading situation has developed. In this particular situation, prices often rally during the first hours of trading offering a good chance to sell, and then collapse.

The next section will contain a number of examples showing zone close/ open patterns with significant probabilities. One of these examples is listed as Pattern #1 which is Gold with a Zone6 close, Zone3 open pattern. This pattern illustrates the principle of a strong close followed by a weak opening. A strong close in Zone6 is typically followed by an opening the next day in Zone4. However, in this pattern prices now open lower in Zone3. With an opening in Zone3, Zone4 Reached is 67%, meaning that 67% of the time prices rally into Zone4 after the open. Zone 4 Resistance is 85%, meaning that 85% of the time prices stop in Zone4. Only 15% of the time did prices have sufficient momentum to rally into Zone5. In other words, Zone4 presents a high probability selling opportunity.

SECTION 5:

USING CLOSE/OPEN PATTERNS

Since today's open and yesterday's close are the most important factors affecting today's price movement, the following zone close/open combinations are possible. Because there are six possibilities for a closing zone, and six possibilities for an opening zone, a total of 36 patterns can be listed as follows:

Zone1 Close Patterns

Zone1 Close	Zone1 Open
Zone1 Close	Zone2 Open
Zone1 Close	Zone3 Open
Zone1 Close	Zone4 Open
Zone1 Close	Zone5 Open
Zone1 Close	Zone6 Open

Zone2 Close Patterns

Zone2 Close	Zone1 Open
Zone2 Close	Zone2 Open
Zone2 Close	Zone3 Open
Zone2 Close	Zone4 Open
Zone2 Close	Zone5 Open
Zone2 Close	Zone6 Open

Zone3 Close Patterns

Zone3 Close	Zone1 Open
Zone3 Close	Zone2 Open
Zone3 Close	Zone3 Open
Zone3 Close	Zone4 Open
Zone3 Close	Zone5 Open
Zone3 Close	Zone6 Open

Zone4 Close Patterns

Zone4 Close	Zone1 Open
Zone4 Close	Zone2 Open
Zone4 Close	Zone3 Open
Zone4 Close	Zone4 Open
Zone4 Close	Zone5 Open
Zone4 Close	Zone6 Open

Zone5 Close Patterns

Zone5 Close	Zone1 Open
Zone5 Close	Zone2 Open
Zone5 Close	Zone3 Open
Zone5 Close	Zone4 Open
Zone5 Close	Zone5 Open
Zone5 Close	Zone6 Open

Zone6 Close Patterns

Zone6 Close	Zone1 Open
Zone6 Close	Zone2 Open
Zone6 Close	Zone3 Open
Zone6 Close	Zone4 Open
Zone6 Close	Zone5 Open
Zone6 Close	Zone6 Open

By using these zone close/open patterns, a multitude of high and low probability zones appear in all markets. On the following pages are ten patterns selected from the probability tables in diverse markets. The light grey bars show how well each zone's resistance holds during the day. The dark grey bars show how well each zone's support holds during the day.

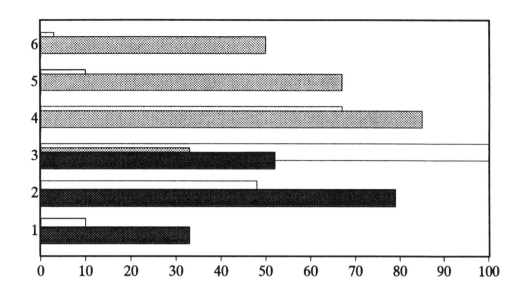

Pattern #1: Gold, Zone6 Close, Zone3 Open

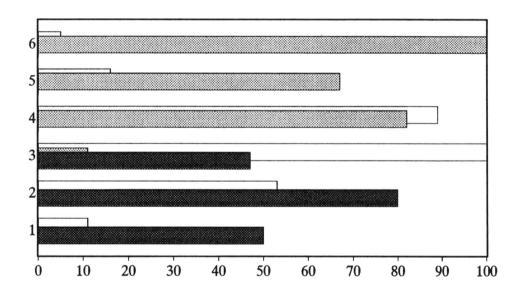

Pattern #2: S&P, Zone6 Close, Zone3 Open

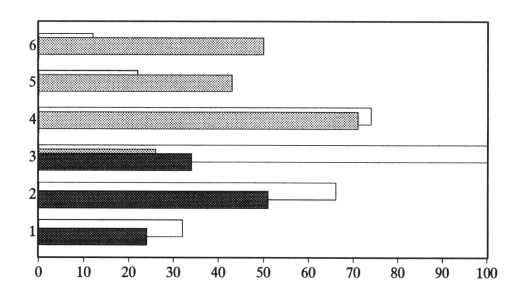

Pattern #3: Treasury Bonds, Zone5 Close, Zone3 Open

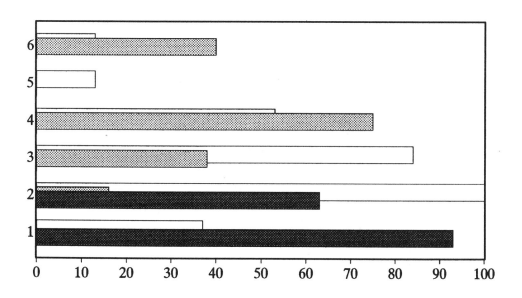

Pattern #4: German Mark, Zone6 Close, Zone2 Open

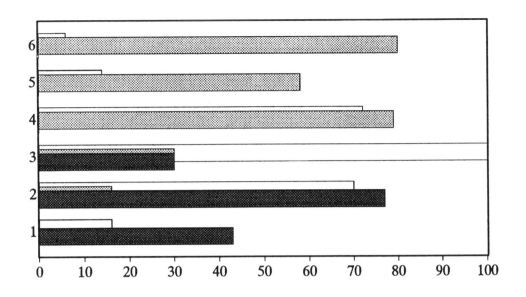

Pattern #5: Japanese Yen, Zone5 Close, Zone3 Open

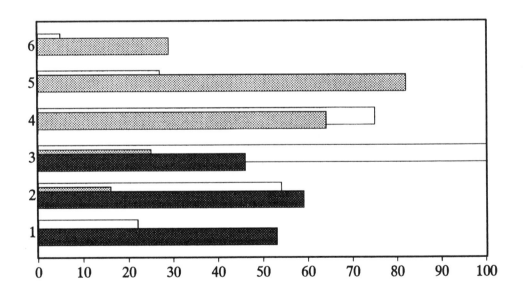

Pattern #6: Swiss Franc, Zone2 Close, Zone3 Open

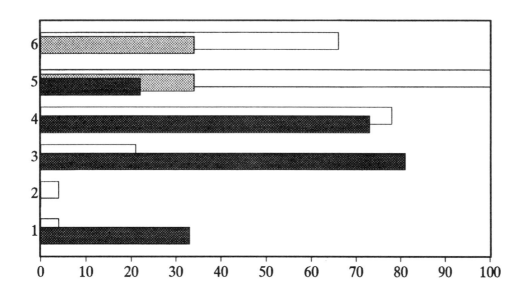

Pattern #7: British Pound, Zone3 Close, Zone5 Open

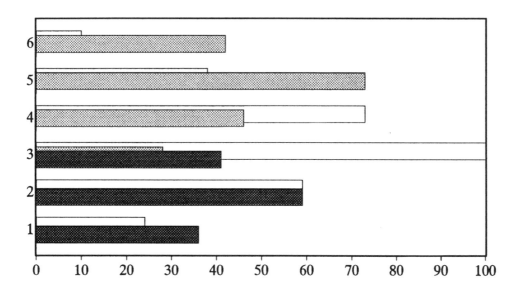

Pattern #8: Soybeans, Zone3 Close, Zone3 Open

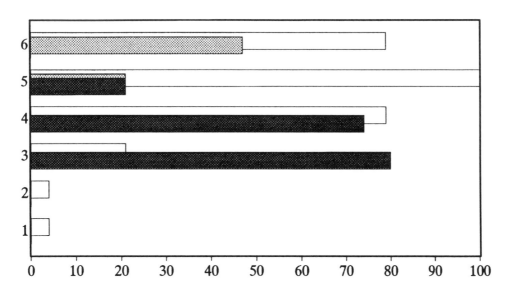

Pattern #9: Live Cattle, Zone5 Close, Zone5 Open

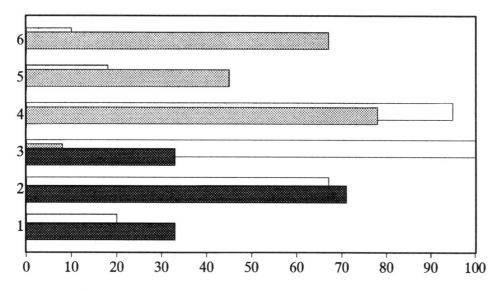

Pattern #10: Sugar, Zone5 Close, Zone3 Open

Some high probability trading situations you should take note of from the zone close/open patterns shown in the previous graphs are:

- Pattern #1: Gold, Zone6 Close, Zone3 Open
  67% Zone4 Reached, 85% Zone4 Resistance

- Pattern #2: S&P, Zone6 Close, Zone3 Open
  89% Zone4 Reached, 82% Zone4 Resistance

- Pattern #3: Treasury Bonds, Zone5 Close, Zone3 Open
  74% Zone4 Reached, 71% Zone4 Resistance

- Pattern #4: German Mark, Zone6 Close, Zone2 Open
  37% Zone1 Reached, 93% Zone1 Support

- Pattern #5: Japanese Yen, Zone5 Close, Zone3 Open
  70% Zone2 Reached, 77% Zone2 Support

- Pattern #6: Swiss Franc, Zone2 Close, Zone3 Open
  27% Zone5 Reached, 82% Zone5 Resistance

- Pattern #7: British Pound, Zone3 Close, Zone5 Open
  78% Zone4 Reached, 73% Zone4 Support

- Pattern #8: Soybeans, Zone3 Close, Zone3 Open
  38% Zone5 Reached, 73% Zone5 Resistance

- Pattern #9: Live Cattle, Zone5 Close, Zone5 Open
  79% Zone4 Reached, 74% Zone4 Support

- Pattern #10: Sugar, Zone5 Close, Zone3 Open
  95% Zone4 Reached, 78% Zone4 Resistance

SECTION 6:

THE PROBABILITY DISTRIBUTION TABLE

The probability distributions can also be expressed in table form. While the graphs allow better visualization of the support and resistance levels, the tables provide a compact format to convey the same information. Below is an example of the probability distribution table for Pattern #1: Gold, Zone6 Close, Zone3 Open:

ZONE 1	ZONE 2	ZONE 3	ZONE 4	ZONE 5	ZONE 6	
		33%	85%	67%	50%	Resist.
33%	79%	52%				Support
10%	48%	100%	67%	10%	3%	Reached

Pattern #1: Gold, Zone6 Close, Zone3 Open

For this pattern, each zone should be interpreted as follows:

Zone1 Support: Prices reach Zone1 10% of the time. If prices reach Zone1, then 33% of the time Zone1 finds support, i.e., Zone1 support is defined as prices rallying to close in a higher zone.

Zone2 Support: Prices reach Zone2 48% of the time. If prices reach Zone2, then 79% of the time Zone2 finds support, i.e., prices will not cross into Zone1.

Zone3 — the opening zone: Prices reach Zone3 100% of the time since by definition this is the opening zone. There is a 52% probability Zone3 finds support, i.e., prices will not cross into Zone2. There is a 33% probability Zone3 finds resistance, i.e., prices will not cross into Zone4.

Zone4 Resistance: Prices reach Zone4 67% of the time. If prices reach Zone4, then 85% of the time Zone4 finds resistance, i.e., prices will not cross into Zone5.

Zone5 Resistance: Prices reach Zone5 10% of the time. If prices reach Zone5, then 67% of the time Zone5 finds resistance, i.e., prices will not cross into Zone6.

Zone6 Resistance: Prices reach Zone6 3% of the time. If prices reach Zone6, then 50% of the time Zone6 finds resistance, i.e., Zone6 resistance is defined as prices breaking to close in a lower zone.

The following are the probability distribution tables for the other nine zone close/open patterns listed in the previous section.

ZONE 1	ZONE 2	ZONE 3	ZONE 4	ZONE 5	ZONE 6	
		11%	82%	67%	100%	Resist.
50%	80%	47%				Support
11%	53%	100%	89%	16%	5%	Reached

Pattern #2: S&P, Zone6 Close, Zone3 Open

ZONE 1	ZONE 2	ZONE 3	ZONE 4	ZONE 5	ZONE 6	
		26%	71%	43%	50%	Resist.
24%	51%	34%				Support
32%	66%	100%	74%	22%	12%	Reached

Pattern #3: Treasury Bonds, Zone5 Close, Zone3 Open

ZONE 1	ZONE 2	ZONE 3	ZONE 4	ZONE 5	ZONE 6	
	16%	38%	75%	0%	40%	Resist.
93%	63%					Support
37%	100%	84%	53%	13%	13%	Reached

Pattern #4: German Mark, Zone6 Close, Zone2 Open

ZONE 1	ZONE 2	ZONE 3	ZONE 4	ZONE 5	ZONE 6	
		30%	79%	58%	80%	Resist.
43%	77%	30%				Support
16%	70%	100%	72%	14%	60%	Reached

Pattern #5: Japanese Yen, Zone5 Close, Zone3 Open

ZONE 1	ZONE 2	ZONE 3	ZONE 4	ZONE 5	ZONE 6	
		25%	64%	82%	29%	Resist.
53%	59%	46%				Support
22%	54%	100%	75%	27%	5%	Reached

Pattern #6: Swiss Franc, Zone2 Close, Zone3 Open

ZONE 1	ZONE 2	ZONE 3	ZONE 4	ZONE 5	ZONE 6	
				34%	34%	Resist.
33%	0%	81%	73%	22%		Support
4%	4%	21%	78%	100%	66%	Reached

Pattern #7: British Pound, Zone3 Close, Zone5 Open

ZONE 1	ZONE 2	ZONE 3	ZONE 4	ZONE 5	ZONE 6	
		28%	46%	73%	42%	Resist.
36%	59%	41%				Support
24%	59%	100%	73%	38%	10%	Reached

Pattern #8: Soybeans, Zone3 Close, Zone3 Open

ZONE 1	ZONE 2	ZONE 3	ZONE 4	ZONE 5	ZONE 6	
				21%	47%	Resist.
33%	79%	80%	74%	21%		Support
10%	48%	21%	79%	100%	79%	Reached

Pattern #9: Live Cattle, Zone6 Close, Zone3 Open

ZONE 1	ZONE 2	ZONE 3	ZONE 4	ZONE 5	ZONE 6	
		8%	78%	45%	67%	Resist.
33%	71%	33%				Support
20%	67%	100%	95%	18%	10%	Reached

Pattern #10: Sugar, Zone5 Close, Zone3 Open

Each market requires 36 such tables, one for each zone close/open pattern. The following two pages contain the probability tables for all 36 zone close/open patterns in the Gold market. Note the Zone6 Close, Zone3 Open table, which is Pattern #1 used in previous examples. Appendix 3 contains identical probability distribution tables for the other major futures markets.

ZONES (1) - (6)   : ZONE(?) CLOSE, ZONE(?) OPEN

(1)	(2)	(3)	(4)	(5)	(6)		
						:	Zone(1) Close, Zone(1) Open
45%	44%	44%	40%	67%	100%	:	Zone Resistance
52%						:	Zone Support
100%	55%	31%	17%	10%	3%	:	Zone Reached
						:	Zone(1) Close, Zone(2) Open
	6%	62%	71%	100%		:	Zone Resistance
62%	46%					:	Zone Support
54%	100%	94%	35%	10%	0%	:	Zone Reached
						:	Zone(1) Close, Zone(3) Open
		39%	72%	77%	50%	:	Zone Resistance
58%	62%	59%				:	Zone Support
15%	41%	100%	62%	16%	4%	:	Zone Reached
						:	Zone(1) Close, Zone(4) Open
			54%	60%	33%	:	Zone Resistance
50%	47%	68%	28%			:	Zone Support
12%	23%	72%	100%	46%	18%	:	Zone Reached
						:	Zone(1) Close, Zone(5) Open
				47%	38%	:	Zone Resistance
	100%	67%	75%	20%		:	Zone Support
0%	7%	20%	80%	100%	53%	:	Zone Reached
						:	Zone(1) Close, Zone(6) Open
					25%	:	Zone Resistance
			100%	67%	25%	:	Zone Support
0%	0%	0%	25%	75%	100%	:	Zone Reached
						:	Zone(2) Close, Zone(1) Open
24%	58%	38%	100%			:	Zone Resistance
48%						:	Zone Support
100%	76%	32%	20%	0%	0%	:	Zone Reached
						:	Zone(2) Close, Zone(2) Open
	29%	33%	56%	57%	67%	:	Zone Resistance
30%	41%					:	Zone Support
59%	100%	71%	47%	21%	9%	:	Zone Reached
						:	Zone(2) Close, Zone(3) Open
		28%	59%	68%	54%	:	Zone Resistance
42%	60%	57%				:	Zone Support
17%	43%	100%	72%	29%	9%	:	Zone Reached
						:	Zone(2) Close, Zone(4) Open
			40%	60%	29%	:	Zone Resistance
50%	50%	76%	30%			:	Zone Support
9%	17%	70%	100%	60%	24%	:	Zone Reached
						:	Zone(2) Close, Zone(5) Open
				53%	62%	:	Zone Resistance
33%	0%	50%	54%	24%		:	Zone Support
18%	18%	35%	76%	100%	47%	:	Zone Reached
						:	Zone(2) Close, Zone(6) Open
					71%	:	Zone Resistance
100%	0%	33%	40%	0%	29%	:	Zone Support
29%	29%	43%	71%	71%	100%	:	Zone Reached
						:	Zone(3) Close, Zone(1) Open
28%	54%	32%	33%	50%	50%	:	Zone Resistance
51%						:	Zone Support
100%	72%	33%	26%	14%	7%	:	Zone Reached
						:	Zone(3) Close, Zone(2) Open
	25%	55%	50%	50%	67%	:	Zone Resistance
47%	25%					:	Zone Support
75%	100%	75%	36%	16%	8%	:	Zone Reached
						:	Zone(3) Close, Zone(3) Open
		25%	58%	62%	36%	:	Zone Resistance
58%	52%	45%				:	Zone Support
26%	55%	100%	75%	31%	12%	:	Zone Reached
						:	Zone(3) Close, Zone(4) Open
			36%	58%	48%	:	Zone Resistance
43%	50%	66%	29%			:	Zone Support
12%	24%	71%	100%	64%	27%	:	Zone Reached
						:	Zone(3) Close, Zone(5) Open
				36%	55%	:	Zone Resistance
33%	25%	29%	50%	24%		:	Zone Support
20%	27%	38%	76%	100%	64%	:	Zone Reached
						:	Zone(3) Close, Zone(6) Open
					44%	:	Zone Resistance
50%	33%	50%	54%	43%	32%	:	Zone Support
6%	9%	18%	38%	68%	100%	:	Zone Reached

Z O N E S   (1) - (6)   : ZONE(?) CLOSE, ZONE(?) OPEN

(1)	(2)	(3)	(4)	(5)	(6)	
						: Zone(4) Close, Zone(1) Open
43%	42%	60%	17%	60%	50%	: Zone Resistance
43%						: Zone Support
100%	57%	33%	13%	11%	4%	: Zone Reached
						: Zone(4) Close, Zone(2) Open
	22%	57%	55%	67%	33%	: Zone Resistance
58%	39%					: Zone Support
61%	100%	78%	34%	15%	5%	: Zone Reached
						: Zone(4) Close, Zone(3) Open
		25%	61%	53%	53%	: Zone Resistance
57%	58%	37%				: Zone Support
27%	63%	100%	76%	28%	13%	: Zone Reached
						: Zone(4) Close, Zone(4) Open
			44%	55%	48%	: Zone Resistance
53%	66%	56%	26%			: Zone Support
11%	33%	74%	100%	56%	25%	: Zone Reached
						: Zone(4) Close, Zone(5) Open
				35%	57%	: Zone Resistance
38%	50%	59%	40%	22%		: Zone Support
10%	19%	47%	78%	100%	65%	: Zone Reached
						: Zone(4) Close, Zone(6) Open
					56%	: Zone Resistance
0%	50%	33%	53%	46%	36%	: Zone Support
5%	11%	16%	35%	64%	100%	: Zone Reached
						: Zone(5) Close, Zone(1) Open
50%	22%	86%	0%	100%		: Zone Resistance
56%						: Zone Support
100%	50%	39%	6%	6%	0%	: Zone Reached
						: Zone(5) Close, Zone(2) Open
	19%	52%	80%	50%	0%	: Zone Resistance
61%	31%					: Zone Support
69%	100%	81%	38%	8%	4%	: Zone Reached
						: Zone(5) Close, Zone(3) Open
		34%	65%	62%	33%	: Zone Resistance
47%	58%	38%				: Zone Support
26%	62%	100%	67%	22%	8%	: Zone Reached
						: Zone(5) Close, Zone(4) Open
			61%	59%	40%	: Zone Resistance
64%	70%	53%	22%			: Zone Support
11%	37%	78%	100%	39%	16%	: Zone Reached
						: Zone(5) Close, Zone(5) Open
				39%	59%	: Zone Resistance
100%	67%	60%	55%	8%		: Zone Support
6%	17%	42%	92%	100%	61%	: Zone Reached
						: Zone(5) Close, Zone(6) Open
					46%	: Zone Resistance
100%	50%	50%	43%	53%	42%	: Zone Support
4%	8%	15%	27%	58%	100%	: Zone Reached
						: Zone(6) Close, Zone(1) Open
56%	25%	33%	0%	0%	50%	: Zone Resistance
33%						: Zone Support
100%	44%	33%	22%	22%	22%	: Zone Reached
						: Zone(6) Close, Zone(2) Open
	28%	62%	88%	0%	0%	: Zone Resistance
70%	31%					: Zone Support
69%	100%	72%	28%	3%	3%	: Zone Reached
						: Zone(6) Close, Zone(3) Open
		33%	85%	67%	50%	: Zone Resistance
33%	79%	52%				: Zone Support
10%	48%	100%	67%	10%	3%	: Zone Reached
						: Zone(6) Close, Zone(4) Open
			64%	53%	53%	: Zone Resistance
33%	72%	66%	30%			: Zone Support
7%	24%	70%	100%	36%	17%	: Zone Reached
						: Zone(6) Close, Zone(5) Open
				38%	67%	: Zone Resistance
	100%	33%	55%	17%		: Zone Support
0%	25%	38%	83%	100%	62%	: Zone Reached
						: Zone(6) Close, Zone(6) Open
					65%	: Zone Resistance
50%	67%	25%	38%	24%	45%	: Zone Support
6%	19%	26%	42%	55%	100%	: Zone Reached

SECTION 7:

TRADE SELECTION AND PLACEMENT

This section concerning trade selection and placement will address the following questions:

1. What probability levels are considered high and low?
2. Where should trades be entered in high support and resistance zones?
3. Where should trades be entered in low support and resistance zones?
4. Where and when should trades be exited?

What Probabilities Are Considered High and Low?

The requisite level of zone probabilities is up to individual preference of risk and frequency of trading desired. Conservative traders can wait for trades where the probabilities are above 70% (or below 30%). More aggressive traders may want to consider trades with probabilities above 60% (or below 40%). Probabilities between 50% to 60% are acceptable when there are additional technical indicators confirming the direction of the trade.

Notice in the probability tables that the opening zone has both a support and resistance probability. These probabilities are included for interest, but in general it is better to wait for prices to extend to a further zone of high/low probability rather than buying or selling in the opening zone.

In addition to the zone support and resistance probabilities, a zone reached probability of 30% or higher is desirable. A designated zone must be reached in order to have the opportunity to make a trade. Therefore, the more frequently the opportune zone is reached, the greater the chance to make a profit.

Where Should Trades Be Entered In High Support/Resistance Zones?

In zones of high probability you buy weakness and sell strength in price (price or better orders). In zones of low probability you buy strength and sell weakness in price (stop orders). Both strategies have merit and the Zone Pattern Probabilities help determine which strategy to employ effectively.

In zones of high support and resistance there are a couple of alternate methods for determining where to place the trade within the zone boundaries. Which method you choose depends on the ability or desirability of watching the market during the day. If you have access to an intraday quote system, you can watch for divergences and %K / %D crossings on a stochastic oscillator.

Stochastics is an oscillator popularized by George Lane. The basic formula is: 1) %K equals today's close minus the low of the last n days, divided by the high of the last n days minus the low of the last n days; 2) %D equals a three-day moving average of the %K. The %K and %D are commonly smoothed by a factor of three to produce a "slow" stochastic. The variable n is the time period used to compute the stochastic. Usually this value is in the range of 5 to 21. Examples in this book will use a 21-bar stochastic since a longer time frame tends to produce smoother results.

The basic stochastic signals occur in two ways. The first is a crossing of the %K and %D lines, combined with a level of %K and %D indicating an oversold or overbought level. Typically, oversold is defined as a %D value of less than 30, and overbought as a value of greater than 70. Utilizing values of 20 and 80 is also common.

The second signal is a divergence between the stochastic and price. A divergence occurs when a market makes a new high or low and the stochastic indicator fails to make a new high or low to confirm. Divergences alone can provide powerful trading signals, but like many technical analysis tools, there are false signals and whipsaws. Divergences occurring in zones of high support and resistance are much more reliable, and provide excellent trading signals.

When using stochastic signals in conjunction with Zone Pattern Probabilities, a valid trading signal occurs when a divergence forms in a zone of high support or resistance and the %K and %D lines cross. A buy signal occurs when a divergence forms in a zone of high support and the %K crosses above the %D. A sell signal occurs when a divergence forms in a zone of high resistance and the %K crosses below the %D.

An example of a stochastic divergence occurring in a zone of high resistance is shown by the graph on the following page. The exact entry point occurs when the %K crosses above the %D, after the divergence. For more information on the application of stochastic oscillators, an excellent source is Computer Analysis of the Futures Markets, by Charles LeBeau and David W. Lucas.

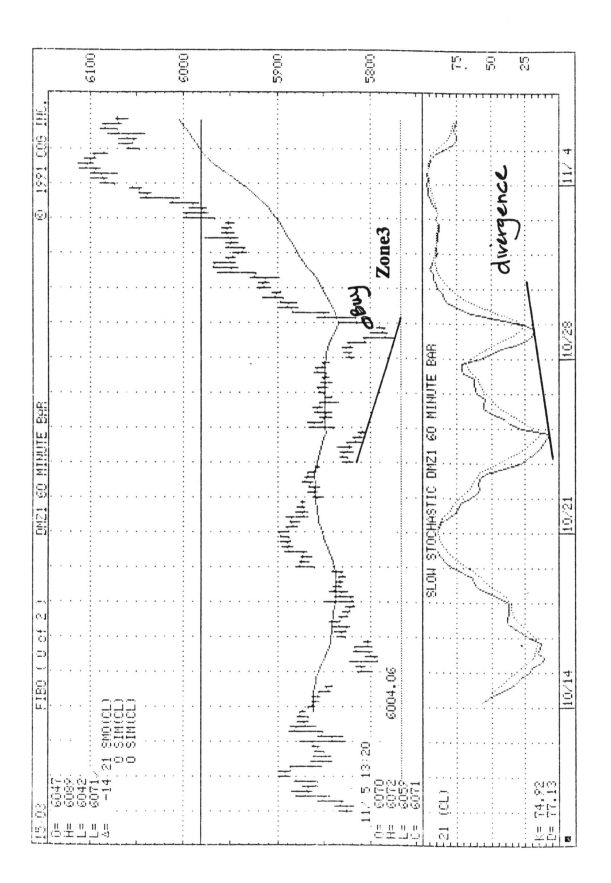

41

If you do not have access to an intraday quote system or prefer not to watch the market during the day, then establish the buy point as follows:

1. Determine the maximum amount you feel comfortable risking on the trade.
2. Determine where your protective stop will be. The stop will always be a few ticks into the next higher zone if selling or the next lower zone if buying.
3. Place your order at the predetermined risk limit's distance from your protective stop.

Consider the following example for selling a Swiss Franc on high resistance.

ZONE 1	ZONE 2	ZONE 3	ZONE 4	ZONE 5	ZONE 6	
	27%	61%	78%	25%	67%	Resist.
38%	35%					Support
65%	100%	73%	30%	5%	4%	Reached

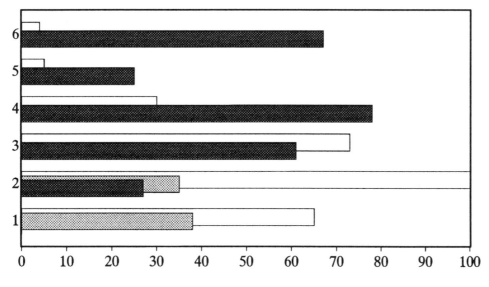

Swiss Franc, Zone4 Close, Zone2 Open

You decide to sell one Swiss Franc in Zone4 on high resistance. First, decide the amount you feel comfortable risking on the trade. Let's assume this amount is $250. Each tick in the Swiss Franc is worth $12.50, therefore

$$250/12.50 = 20 \text{ ticks}$$

you are willing to risk. Next, determine where to place your protective stop. Since you are selling high resistance in Zone4, your protective stop should be placed a few ticks into Zone5. Assume the Zone4 / Zone5 boundary is at 6900. You would place a protective buy stop at 6902. Lastly, compute the distance from the protective stop which will risk the predetermined amount. In this case,

$$6902 - 20 = 6882.$$

Therefore, you would place your sell order at 6882 and a protective buy stop at 6902. Using this method you are never risking more per trade than a predetermined amount which should be within your risk threshold.

Trades with high resistance and support can be graphically displayed as follows:

Orders in Zones of High Resistance

Zone6 :

Zone5 : protective stop

HIGH RESISTANCE   Zone4 : sell order

---

current price   Zone3 :

Zone2 :

Zone1 :

Orders in Zones of High Support

Zone6 :

Zone5 :

---

current price   Zone4 :

HIGH SUPPORT   Zone3 : buy order

Zone2 : protective stop

Zone1 :

Where Should Trades Be Entered In Low Support / Resistance Zones?

In zones of low support and resistance you are trading price breakouts using stop orders. Breakouts are a well-known technique for trading futures. You are buying when prices prove they can move higher, and selling when prices prove they can move lower. Unfortunately there are also false breakouts when prices confirm a direction, but then turn and reverse sharply in the other direction. The ideal would be to find an indicator which predicts when the price breakout will be successful.

This is exactly the purpose of Zone Pattern Probability Analysis. It gives the probability of a successful breakout in the form of low support and low resistance numbers. For example, look at the following probability table for Gold with a Zone3 Close and Zone5 open.

ZONE 1	ZONE 2	ZONE 3	ZONE 4	ZONE 5	ZONE 6	
				36%	55%	Resist.
33%	25%	29%	50%	24%		Support
20%	27%	38%	76%	100%	64%	Reached

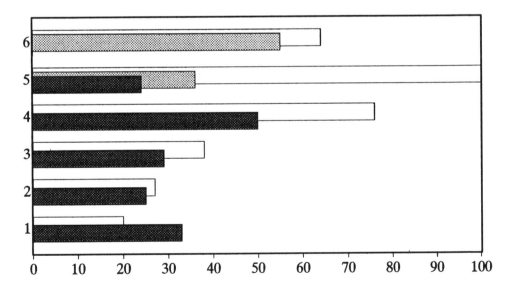

Gold, Zone3 Close, Zone5 Open

45

Notice the Zone3 support of only 29%. This zone support means that historically when prices reach Zone3, then only 29% of the time prices stopped in Zone3. The other 71% of the time prices reached Zone2. <u>You want to enter the trade as soon as prices enter the zone of low support or resistance</u>. In this example, you enter a stop order to sell as soon as prices enter into Zone3. Additionally, notice the low zone support numbers in Zone2 and Zone1. This is a powerful trade because multiple, adjacent zones are showing low support.

After your stop order is filled, you want to place a protective stop. A protective stop should be placed in the next adjacent zone. In this example of selling on low support in Zone3, you should place your protective stop in Zone4. The exact placement of the stop should be determined by the amount you feel comfortable risking on the trade. For example, assume the Zone3 / Zone4 boundary is at 350.00. Your sell stop order is filled at 349.80. Assume you feel comfortable risking $250 for the trade. Since one tick in Gold is worth $10 then you will risk

$$250/10 = 2.50 \text{ ticks.}$$

Therefore, you will place your protective stop at

$$349.80 + 2.50 = 352.30.$$

Often, however, with examples showing tremendous price weakness such as Gold with a Zone3 Close, Zone5 Open, prices drop so quickly that it is possible to place a breakeven stop shortly after your initial entry. These are oftentimes high profit days with minimal risk.

Graphically, selling in zones of low support or buying in zones of low resistance appears as follows:

Orders in Zones of Low Support

Zone6 :
_____

Zone5 :
_____

current price   Zone4 : protective stop
_____

LOW SUPPORT   Zone3 : sell stop order
_____

Zone2 :
_____

Zone1 :

Orders in Zones of Low Resistance

Zone6 :
_____

Zone5 :
_____

LOW RESISTANCE   Zone4 : buy stop order
_____

current price   Zone3 : protective stop
_____

Zone2 :
_____

Zone1 :

Where And When Should Trades Be Exited?

There are three strategies to determine when to exit a trade. Which exit method you employ depends on your time frame preference for day trading or position trading. Use the technique which corresponds to your individual preference.

- Day Trading: Exiting in Zones of High Support/Resistance

If prices reach a zone of high probability during the day, exit the trade. Consider the example below for the Japanese Yen with a Zone5 Close, Zone3 Open.

ZONE 1	ZONE 2	ZONE 3	ZONE 4	ZONE 5	ZONE 6	
		30%	79%	58%	80%	Resist.
43%	77%	30%				Support
16%	70%	100%	72%	14%	6%	Reached

Japanese Yen, Zone5 Close, Zone3 Open

Assume you sell Zone4 on high resistance of 79% and now prices have reached Zone2 with a high support of 77%. Zone2 would be a strategic intraday location to exit the trade since there is a 77% chance that Zone2 will be the low zone for the day.

- Day Trading: Exiting Market On Close (MOC)

Consider the example below for the Japanese Yen with a Zone4 Close, Zone4 Open. Assume you buy in Zone2 on high support of 68%. Prices then begin to rally into Zone3 and then Zone4. However, notice that Zone3 and Zone4 and even Zone5 and Zone6 do not have significant zone resistance probabilities. Therefore, since there is no clear exit zone indicated by the probabilities, exit the trade at the close (MOC).

ZONE 1	ZONE 2	ZONE 3	ZONE 4	ZONE 5	ZONE 6	
			44%	53%	53%	Resist.
58%	68%	54%	28%			Support
10%	33%	72%	100%	56%	26%	Reached

Japanese Yen, Zone4 Close, Zone4 Open

- Position Trading

If you wish to hold overnight and position trade, determine at the close if the trade is profitable. If so, then continue to hold the trade if it is in the direction of the trend. In this way you only hold trades overnight when they are in the direction of the trend and have already proved profitable. Bruce Babcock makes the following statement in his book The Business One Irwin Guide to Trading Systems: "The late Frankie Joe was one of the best and most famous of big-time speculators in the 1970s and 1980s. He had a very simple approach to trading. He once confided that his real secret was never to go home with a loss. That means he never wanted to hold a position after the close unless it was already profitable. Frankie Joe's money management rule is the ultimate in cutting losses short. It sounds radical and unrealistic, but it makes a great deal of sense, especially for a short-term trader. If you study your successful trades, you will find that many, if not most, were immediately profitable and never were behind on a closing basis. Thus, you have little to lose and a great deal to gain by exiting losers as quickly as possible."

Combining position trading with short-term techniques can provide the best of both worlds: the potential for large gain with small risk. To apply this technique you should trade at least two contracts per initial position. The technique exits half of the entry amount on an intraday zone of high probability, and then holds half of the entry amount for a position trade. Section 8: Pattern Examples will show specific illustrations where this technique is applied. Consider the following example for the German Mark with a Zone6 Close, Zone2 open. Assume the trend of the German mark over the last few months is up.

49

ZONE 1	ZONE 2	ZONE 3	ZONE 4	ZONE 5	ZONE 6	
	16%	38%	75%	0%	40%	Resist.
93%	63%					Support
37%	100%	84%	53%	13%	13%	Reached

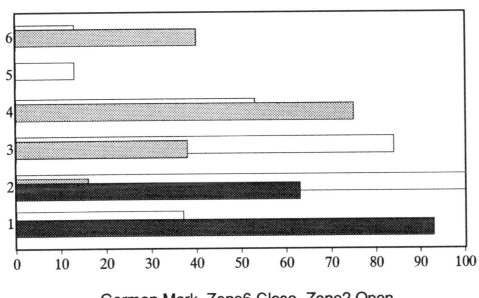

German Mark, Zone6 Close, Zone2 Open

Prices open in Zone2 and you buy two contracts on a price dip into Zone1 with a zone support of 93%. During the day prices begin to rally and reach Zone4. Since Zone4 has a 75% zone resistance you decide to exit one contract for a profit in this zone. You hold the other contract at least until the close. At the close, prices have dipped back into Zone3, but since you purchased your contract in Zone1, you still have a profit. Therefore, since the trend is up and your position is profitable at the close, you hold one contract for a position trade.

This technique provides a number of benefits. First, your initial purchase in Zone1 has a small "daytrading" risk. Stops between $200-$250 are typical. Second, you have already taken some profits as prices reached high resistance in Zone4. This provides a cushion if prices should move adversely when holding overnight. Lastly, at the close your position is profitable, and you are trading with the trend and conforming to proven trading rules. This is perhaps the best technique to find trades with exceptional risk/reward ratios.

SECTION 8:

PATTERN EXAMPLES

Section 5 contained ten high zone probability patterns. This section will analyze in greater detail the probability tables for each of these patterns. The market examples include Gold, S&P, Treasury Bonds, German Mark, Japanese Yen, Swiss Franc, British Pound, Soybeans, Live Cattle and Sugar. Appendix 3 contains the probability distribution tables for all the markets. The examples represent only a small subset of profitable zone patterns.

Pattern #1: Gold, Zone6 Close, Zone3 Open

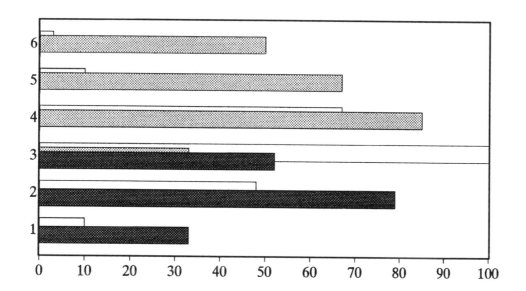

ZONE 1	ZONE 2	ZONE 3	ZONE 4	ZONE 5	ZONE 6	
		33%	85%	67%	50%	Resist.
33%	79%	52%				Support
10%	48%	100%	67%	10%	3%	Reached

This first pattern was discussed briefly in Section 4. Notice Zone4 with a 85% resistance and a 67% zone reached. Again, Zone5 also provides a selling opportunity with a resistance of 67%, but this is less than Zone4's resistance of 85% and Zone5 is only reached 10% of the time. Zone4 is the clear choice to be a seller. On the support side, Zone2 provides a 79% probability of support. It is clear that if you go short in Zone4, you should take some profits if prices enter Zone2. Those trading multiple contracts can exit half the position and wait to see if prices cross into Zone1 which has only a 33% support.

A Zone6 Close, Zone3 Open provides a nice chance to hop aboard a position trade if the market is trending in either direction. If prices are trending up trade as follows: 1) buy in Zone2, 2) place a protective stop in Zone1, 3) take half of the profits if prices reach Zone4 and hold the other half for a position trade. If prices are trending down trade as follows: 1) sell in Zone4, 2) place a protective stop in Zone5, 3) take half of the profits in Zone2 and hold the other half for a position trade.

Pattern #2: S&P, Zone6 Close, Zone3 Open

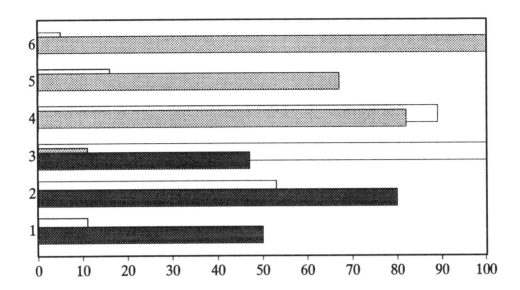

ZONE 1	ZONE 2	ZONE 3	ZONE 4	ZONE 5	ZONE 6	
		11%	82%	67%	100%	Resist.
50%	80%	47%				Support
11%	53%	100%	89%	16%	5%	Reached

The zones of extreme probabilities include Zone2 support of 80%, Zone4 resistance of 82%, Zone5 resistance of 67% and Zone6 resistance of 100%. Notice that prices find high resistance in each of the zones above the opening price. To determine the zone in which to place a sell order, look at the percentage each zone is reached. Zone4 is reached 89%, Zone5 is reached 16% and Zone6 is reached only 5%. In other words you have a chance to sell in Zone4 89% of the time, compared with only 16% of the time in Zone5 and 5% of the time in Zone6. Since Zone4 resistance probability is a whopping 82%, look to sell a contract in Zone4.

When selling strength on high probability, place a protective stop a few ticks into the adjacent zone — in this case Zone5.

The exit is determined by the time frame of trading. If day trading — exit if prices reach Zone2 since the zone support is 80%. If prices never reach Zone2, exit the trade Market on Close. If position trading, hold the trade overnight if it is in the direction of the trend and profitable at the close.

Pattern #3: Treasury Bonds, Zone5 Close, Zone3 Open

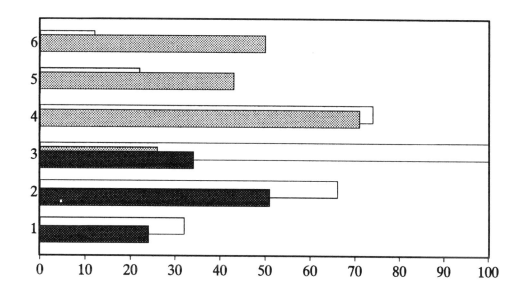

ZONE 1	ZONE 2	ZONE 3	ZONE 4	ZONE 5	ZONE 6	
		26%	71%	43%	50%	Resist.
24%	51%	34%				Support
32%	66%	100%	74%	22%	12%	Reached

The two zones with acceptable probabilities are Zone1 with 24% support and Zone4 with 71% resistance. Notice that you have the probability to sell Zone4 about twice as often as Zone1 since Zone4 reached is 74% and Zone1 is only 32%. You can place a sell order in Zone4 or place a sell stop order as prices enter into Zone1. The ideal trade would be to sell Zone4 and then have the price reach Zone1.

If you sell Zone4, a protective buy stop should be placed a few ticks into Zone5. If you sell on a stop in Zone1, place a money management protective buy stop in Zone2.

Notice that there are no zones of high support indicating a location where prices are likely to stop. Thus you should exit the position on the close if daytrading. If position trading, hold the trade overnight if it is in the direction of the trend and profitable at the close.

Pattern #4: German Mark, Zone6 Close, Zone2 Open

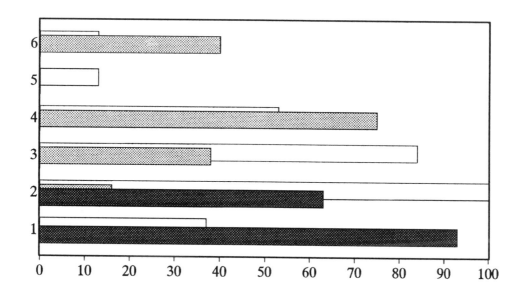

ZONE 1	ZONE 2	ZONE 3	ZONE 4	ZONE 5	ZONE 6	
	16%	38%	75%	0%	40%	Resist.
93%	63%					Support
37%	100%	84%	53%	13%	13%	Reached

Zones of high/low probability include Zone1 with a support of 93%, Zone4 with a resistance of 75%, and Zone5 with a resistance of 0%. Try to visualize how a typical Zone6 close, Zone2 open day might trade. Prices rallied strongly yesterday to close in Zone6. Overnight there is a substantial break in prices and the open is now in Zone2. After the open there is a continuing drop of prices from Zone2 into Zone1. Then prices find strong support at 93% and begin to rally. From Zone1 prices rally to Zone4 where they encounter a significant 75% resistance. Zone4/Zone5 boundary is a strategic resistance point. If prices can rally through this border, then prices have always rallied to reach Zone6, and 60% of the time (100%-40%) prices have closed above the Zone6 boundary.

Consider the following trades. If prices break to Zone1 first, go long on Zone1 support of 93%. Consider exiting this trade in Zone4 with a resistance of 75%. However, also notice that if prices breach the Zone4 upper boundary that

Zone5 resistance is 0% and Zone6 is only 40%. This is an ideal situation if trading multiple contracts. Exit half the position as prices reach Zone4 and hold the other half to see if prices can breach the Zone4 boundary and rally to close in Zone6.

Another scenario to consider is that prices never reach Zone1. Suppose instead that prices rally to Zone4. In this case consider going short in Zone4 on 75% resistance. The protective stop would normally be placed a few ticks into Zone5. However, since Zone5 resistance is 0% and Zone6 resistance is only 40%, you should not only cover the short position as the price reaches Zone5, but also reverse to a long position.

Pattern #5: Japanese Yen, Zone5 Close, Zone3 Open

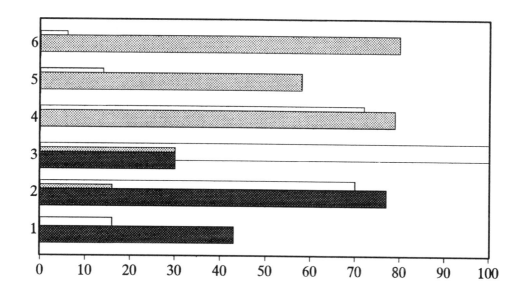

ZONE 1	ZONE 2	ZONE 3	ZONE 4	ZONE 5	ZONE 6	
		30%	79%	58%	80%	Resist.
43%	77%	30%				Support
16%	70%	100%	72%	14%	6%	Reached

Zones of high probability include Zone2 with a support of 77%, Zone4 with a resistance of 79% and Zone6 with a resistance of 80%. Zone2 and Zone4 allow frequent trading with zone reached percentages above 70%. Zone6 trades offer a high probability but occur very rarely with a zone reached of only 6%. Buying a contract in Zone2 and selling a contract in Zone4 are both frequently occurring, high probability trades. If day trading, the selected trade should be determined by whichever zone is reached first during the day. For example, if Zone2 is reached first, become a buyer for the day. If Zone4 is reached first, become a seller for the day. If you buy Zone2, profits should then be taken if prices reach Zone4 since there is a 79% resistance. If you sell Zone4, profits should be taken in Zone2 with a support of 77%.

If trading for the longer term, determine the direction of the market trend. If a strong trend exists, this is an excellent chance to hop aboard. If the market

trend is up, only buy in Zone2. If prices then rally and the trade is profitable, hold overnight rather than exiting the position in Zone4. (If trading multiple contracts consider exiting some of the position at a Zone4 profit and holding some of the position for the longer term). If the market trend is down, only consider selling in Zone4. If prices continue to slide and the trade is profitable, hold overnight rather than exiting the position in Zone2. (Again, if trading multiple contracts, consider covering some of the position at a Zone2 profit and hold some of the position for the longer term.)

Pattern #6: Swiss Franc, Zone2 Close, Zone3 Open

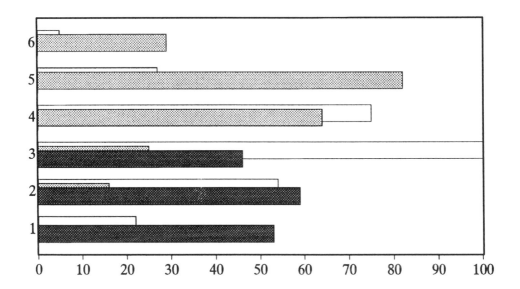

ZONE 1	ZONE 2	ZONE 3	ZONE 4	ZONE 5	ZONE 6	
		25%	64%	82%	29%	Resist.
53%	59%	46%				Support
22%	54%	100%	75%	27%	5%	Reached

The best trade from the zone probabilities is to sell Zone5 with 82% resistance. Notice also Zone2 with 59% support, Zone4 with 64% resistance and Zone6 with 29% resistance. It is important to analyze the percentage of time each zone is reached. Zone5, while providing an excellent trading opportunity, has a zone reached of only 27%. Patient traders can wait for these high probability opportunities which occur less than a third of the time. A more frequently occurring trade is to sell Zone4 with 64% resistance and a zone reached of 75%. Since the probability is not as high as Zone5, you may want to require confirmation from an additional technical indicator such as a momentum divergence on a stochastic oscillator. A momentum divergence with a 64% resistance and a zone reached of 75% provides for a pretty good trade.

Since Zone2 support is under 60%, pass on any trades in this zone. More aggressive traders can elect to buy Zone2 if other technical indicators confirm

prices bottoming in Zone2. Zone5, as mentioned earlier, provides an extremely high probability that prices will stop in this zone, but this occurs less frequently than Zone4.

Stops on all trades where you are buying weakness or selling strength should be placed a few ticks beyond the border into the next zone. Notice that when prices break through Zone5 into Zone6 (Zone6 is reached only 5% of the time), prices closed above the Zone6 boundary 71% (100%—29%) of the time.

Pattern #7: British Pound, Zone3 Close, Zone5 Open

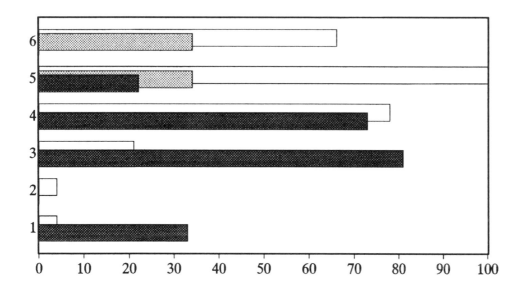

	ZONE 1	ZONE 2	ZONE 3	ZONE 4	ZONE 5	ZONE 6	
					34%	34%	Resist.
	33%	0%	81%	73%	22%		Support
	4%	4%	21%	78%	100%	66%	Reached

The two zones of major interest are Zone4 with a zone support of 73% and a zone reached of 78% and Zone6 with a zone resistance of 34% and a zone reached of 66%. Zone3 also provides extremely high support but with a zone reached of only 21%. These high support and low resistance percentages, along with the high zone reached percentages of Zone4 and Zone6 indicate that the majority of time you encounter this pattern, you should plan to go long during the day.

A crucial price location where the long perspective changes is at the Zone2/Zone3 boundary. These critical boundaries are snapping points in the market. If prices cross into Zone2 then 0% of the time prices stopped in Zone2, and only 33% of the time prices closed above Zone1. Seeing these probabilities helps to maintain discipline in using stops. If you trade without stops, and prices cross the Zone2/Zone3 boundary while you are long, you are likely to be in for a big loss.

Pattern #8: Soybeans, Zone3 Close, Zone3 Open

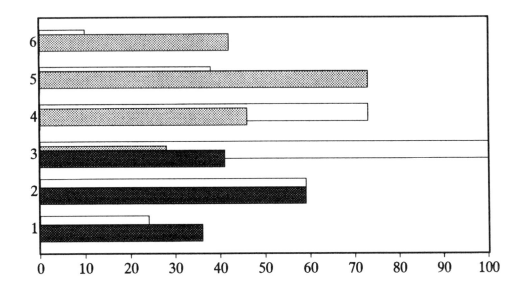

ZONE 1	ZONE 2	ZONE 3	ZONE 4	ZONE 5	ZONE 6	
		28%	46%	73%	42%	Resist.
36%	59%	41%				Support
24%	59%	100%	73%	38%	10%	Reached

By now you should be becoming familiar with determining which zones are of interest and visualizing from the probabilities how prices might trade during the day. Certainly one good trade in this example is to sell a Zone5 with 73% resistance. Another possible trade is to sell as prices enter Zone1 on a stop order. Zone2 is below the 60% probability threshold with a support of 59%, and Zone6 is below this threshold as well with a resistance of 42% (100%-42% = 58%). Aggressive traders can still consider trading these zones if there are additional strong technical indicators confirming price direction.

Pattern #9: Live Cattle, Zone5 Close, Zone5 Open

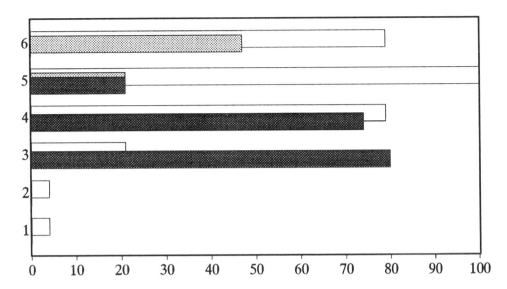

ZONE 1	ZONE 2	ZONE 3	ZONE 4	ZONE 5	ZONE 6	
				21%	47%	Resist.
0%	0%	80%	74%	21%		Support
4%	4%	21%	79%	100%	79%	Reached

Where is the "snapping" point for Live Cattle with a Zone5 Close, Zone5 Open? In Zone3 prices have 80% support, but if prices cross into Zone2 there is historically a 0% Zone2 support and a 0% Zone1 support. Until prices cross into Zone2, look to be long for the day since Zone3 has a zone support of 80% and Zone4 has a zone support of 74%. Since Zone4 reached is much more frequent than Zone3 (79% versus 21%), look to buy in Zone4 rather than waiting for prices to enter Zone3. Normally, if a buyer in Zone4, you should place the protective stop a few ticks into Zone3. However, since Zone3 still has an 80% resistance, and since the Zone2/Zone3 boundary is such a critical point, it is preferable to place the protective stop a few ticks into Zone2. Profits from any purchase in Zone4 can either be taken in Zone6 or held to the close. Notice there is a high probability prices will reach Zone6 (79% zone reached), but only a 47% chance prices will return to close below Zone6.

Pattern #10: Sugar, Zone5 Close, Zone3 Open

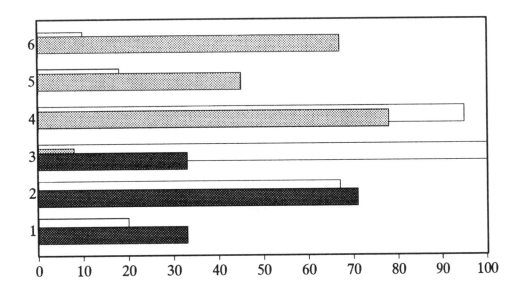

ZONE 1	ZONE 2	ZONE 3	ZONE 4	ZONE 5	ZONE 6	
		8%	78%	45%	67%	Resist.
33%	71%	33%				Support
20%	67%	100%	95%	18%	10%	Reached

Notice the high support/resistance zone probabilities in Zone2 and Zone4, as well as the high percentages these zones are reached. Zone4 is reached 95% of the time and has a 78% resistance! This is a high probability trade you will have the opportunity to make on nearly every Zone5 Close, Zone3 Open trading day. A protective stop should be placed a few ticks beyond the Zone4/Zone5 boundary. If trading multiple contracts, half of the profit should be taken if prices reach Zone2 with a 71% zone support. The other half should be held in case prices enter Zone1 since there is only 33% support after prices cross the Zone1 boundary. If trading only one contract, it is up to the trader to decide whether to exit in Zone2 or hold to see if prices will penetrate Zone1.

If market prices are trending down, this is an excellent trading day to enter a position trade. (Also, if already holding a short position, this provides an excellent opportunity to add to the position.) Look how Zone Pattern Probability

Analysis helps you hop aboard a position trade with a minimal amount of risk. Enter the market in Zone4 with a 78% resistance probability. Even though this is a position trade, the protective stop will be at the Zone4/Zone5 boundary so the risk is an amount common to day traders and much lower than for typical position traders. When prices enter Zone2 exit half the position and take some immediate profits. If prices close in Zone2 or enter Zone1, then the position will close profitably for the day and you can hold overnight — having risked a minimal amount of capital and having already taken some profits as a cushion. This provides for an outstanding risk/reward ratio.

SECTION 9:

TRADING EXAMPLES

The following are examples of trades selected using the probability distribution tables. The examples have been selected to illustrate a diverse range of trading situations you may encounter using Zone Pattern Probability Analysis. Since these examples use CQG intraday quotes, orders buying weakness and selling strength were initiated on momentum divergences in zones of high support and high resistance. For those traders not having access to an intraday quote system, placement of entry orders in zones of high support and high resistance can be determined by deciding the amount of desired trade risk as described in Section 7.

The graphs are printed courtesy of CQG Inc. For each trade refer to Appendix 3 for the appropriate probability tables.

December Crude Oil (11/01)
Pattern: Zone5 Close, Zone5 Open

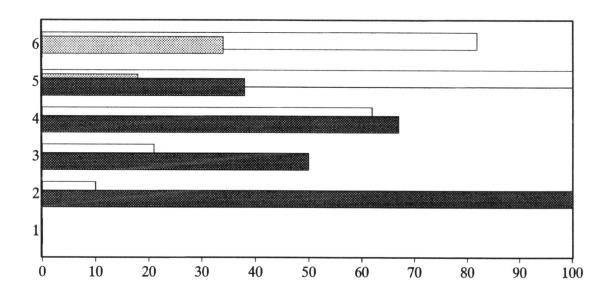

ZONE 1	ZONE 2	ZONE 3	ZONE 4	ZONE 5	ZONE 6	
0%	100%	50%	67%	38%		Support
				18%	34%	Resist.
0%	21%	64%	62%	100%	82%	Reached

Trade Analysis: Buy on a price dip in Zone4 with support of 67%, or buy on a stop order as prices enter Zone6. Since Zone4 is never reached, the stop order is filled in Zone6.

Trade Decision: Buy Zone6 on 34% resistance on a stop order.

Trade Result: Buy order is placed at 23.56. Trade is exited on the close at 23.82.

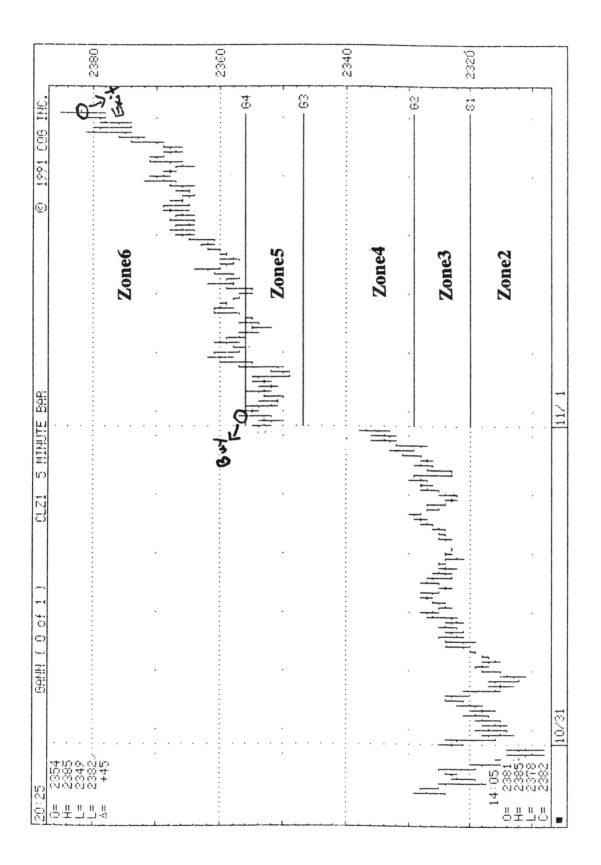

December German Mark (11/06)
Pattern: Zone3 Close, Zone4 Open

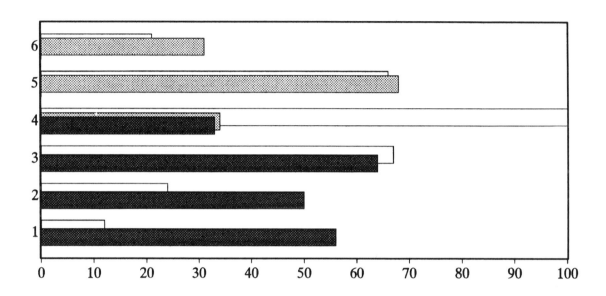

ZONE 1	ZONE 2	ZONE 3	ZONE 4	ZONE 5	ZONE 6	
			34%	68%	31%	Resist.
56%	50%	64%	36%	33%		Support
12%	24%	67%	100%	66%	21%	Reached

Trade Analysis: If prices reach Zone5 first, sell on 68% resistance. If prices reach Zone3 first, buy on 64% support. Since prices reach Zone5 first, sell on the momentum divergence. Trade is exited when prices reach Zone3 since this is a zone of high support.

Trade Decision: Sell Zone5 on 68% resistance and momentum divergence.

Trade Result: A sell order is placed at 6100. Trade is exited in Zone3 at 6064.

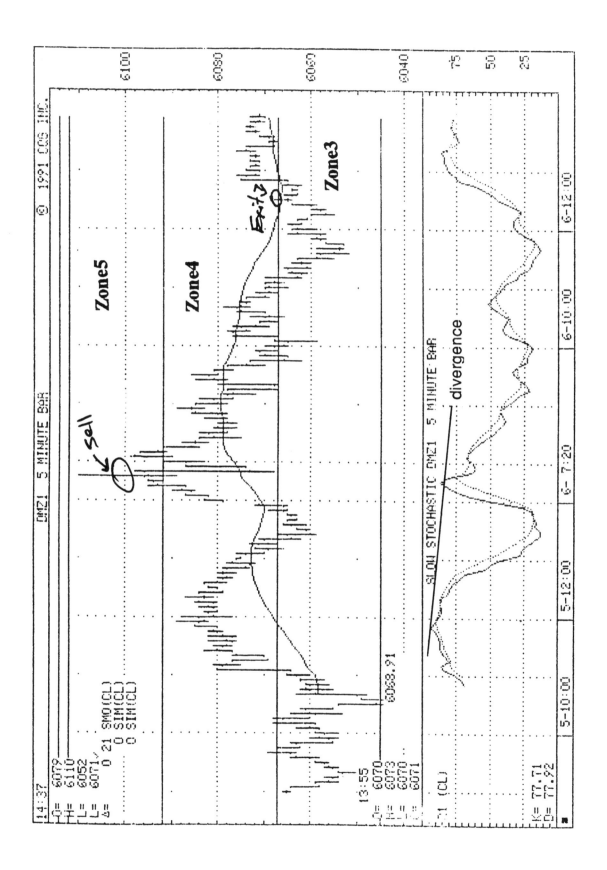

January Crude Oil (11/14)
Pattern: Zone3 Close, Zone3 Open

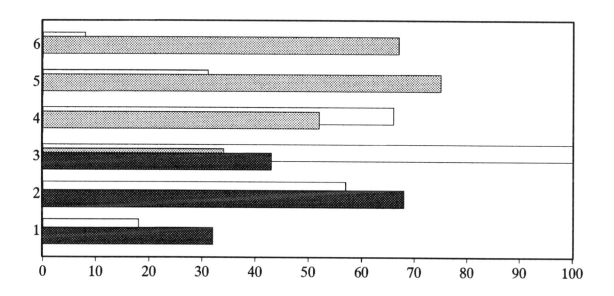

ZONE 1	ZONE 2	ZONE 3	ZONE 4	ZONE 5	ZONE 6	
		34%	52%	75%	67%	Resist.
32%	68%	43%				Support
18%	57%	100%	66%	31%	8%	Reached

Trade Analysis: Look to either buy Zone2 on 68% support or sell Zone5 on 75% resistance. Since prices enter Zone2 first, place a buy order on the momentum divergence. A protective sell stop should be placed a few ticks into Zone1. Zone1 is also a stop and reverse point to a short position since there is only 32% zone support.

Trade Decision: Buy Zone2 on 68% support and momentum divergence.

Trade Result: Buy order is placed at 22.00. Trade is exited on the close at 22.37.

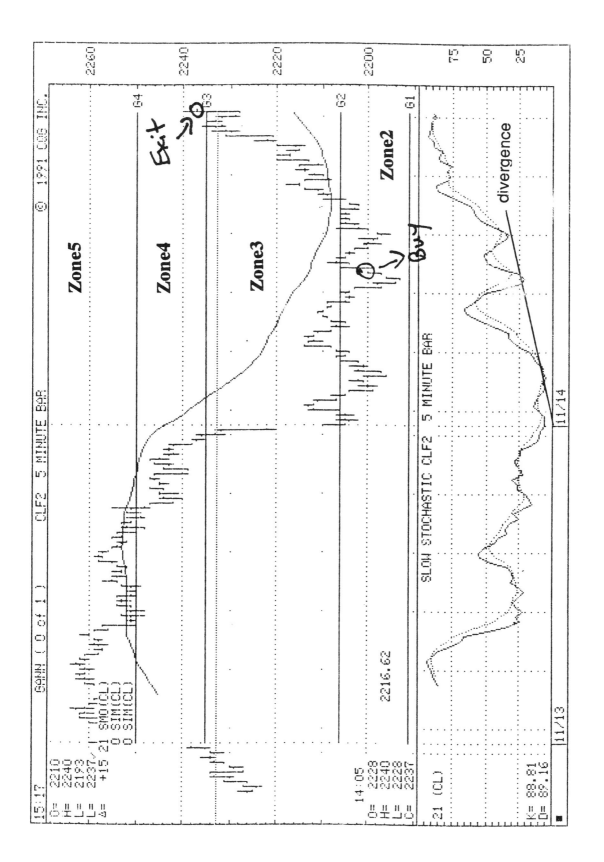

74

December German Mark (11/29)
Pattern: Zone6 Close, Zone4 Open

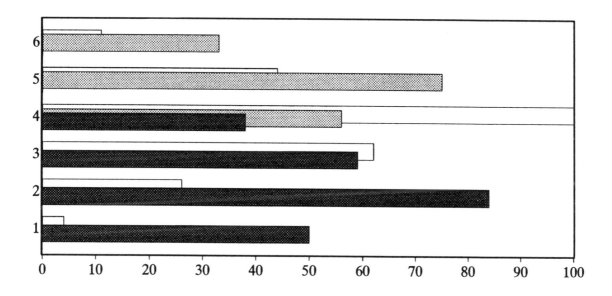

ZONE 1	ZONE 2	ZONE 3	ZONE 4	ZONE 5	ZONE 6	
			56%	75%	33%	Resist.
50%	84%	59%	38%			Support
4%	26%	62%	100%	44%	11%	Reached

Trade Analysis: Possible trades to consider are: 1) a buy order in Zone2 on high support, 2) a sell order in Zone5 on high resistance, 3) a buy stop order in Zone6 on low resistance. Since Zone5 is reached first, place a sell order in Zone5. If prices reach Zone6, stop and reverse to a long position since Zone6 has a resistance level of only 33%.

Trade Decision: Sell Zone5 on 75% resistance. Stop and reverse to long when prices breach Zone6.

Trade Result: Sell order is placed at 5843. Short trade is stopped and long trade is entered at 5862. Exit is on the close.

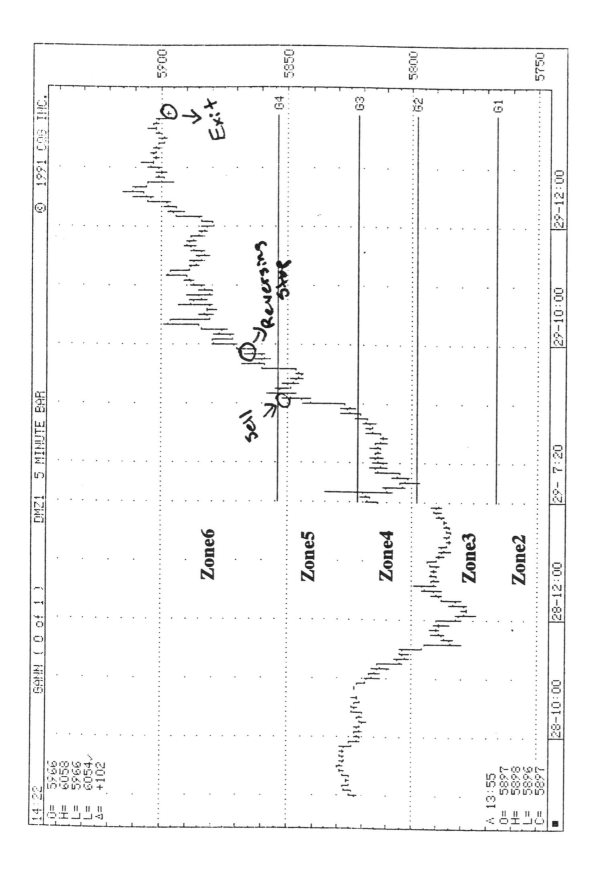

December German Mark (11/04)
Pattern: Zone6 Close, Zone4 Open

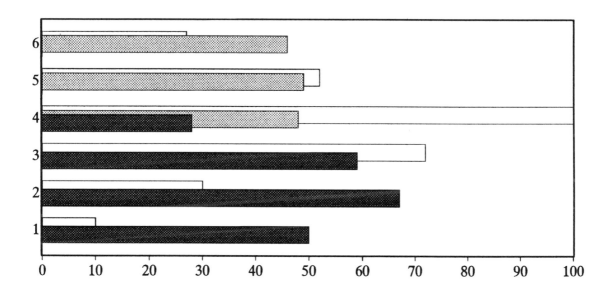

ZONE 1	ZONE 2	ZONE 3	ZONE 4	ZONE 5	ZONE 6	
			56%	75%	33%	Resist.
50%	84%	59%	38%			Support
4%	26%	62%	100%	44%	11%	Reached

Trade Analysis: Zone5 with a high resistance of 75%, combined with a momentum divergence provides an excellent selling opportunity. Place a protective stop in Zone6 and reverse to a long position since Zone6 resistance is only 33%.

Trade Decision: Sell Zone5 on 75% resistance and momentum divergence. Stop and reverse to a long position if prices reach Zone6.

Trade Results: Sell order is placed in Zone5 at 6100. Trade is exited on the close.

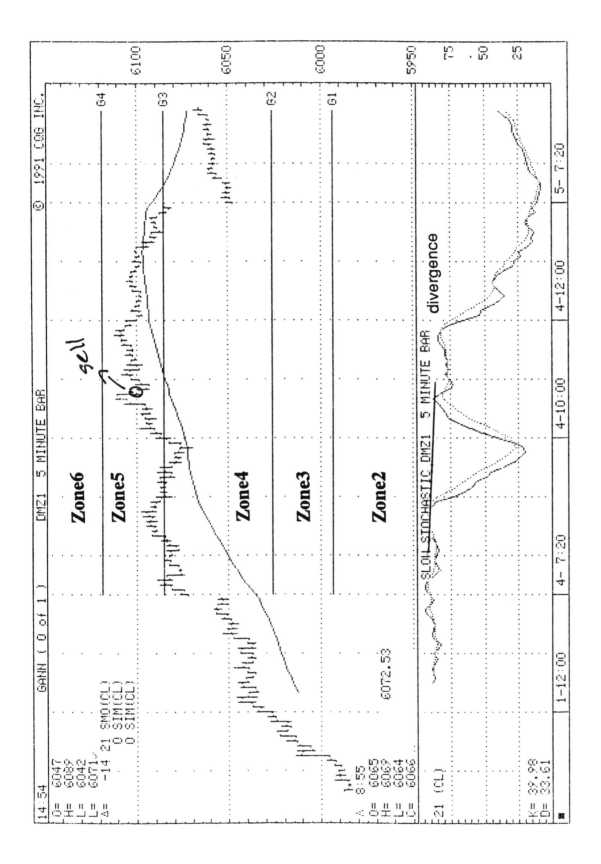

(C) Copyright 1991 CQG INC.

December Gold (10/25)
Pattern: Zone3 Close, Zone5 Open

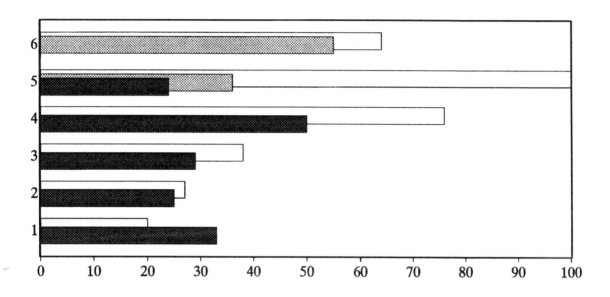

ZONE 1	ZONE 2	ZONE 3	ZONE 4	ZONE 5	ZONE 6	
				36%	55%	Resist.
33%	25%	29%	50%	24%		Support
20%	27%	38%	76%	100%	64%	Reached

Trade Analysis: Multiple low probabilities indicate definite weakness as prices cross into the lower zones. Zone Pattern Probability Analysis helps determine that the border of Zone3 is a strategic point at which prices should break significantly. Since this trade is late in the day, prices do not have time to collapse. As a result, it would be better to hold this trade overnight rather than exit on the close.

Trade Decision: Sell Zone3 on 29% support on a stop order.

Trade Result: Sell stop order is placed in Zone3 at 3634. Trade is held overnight.

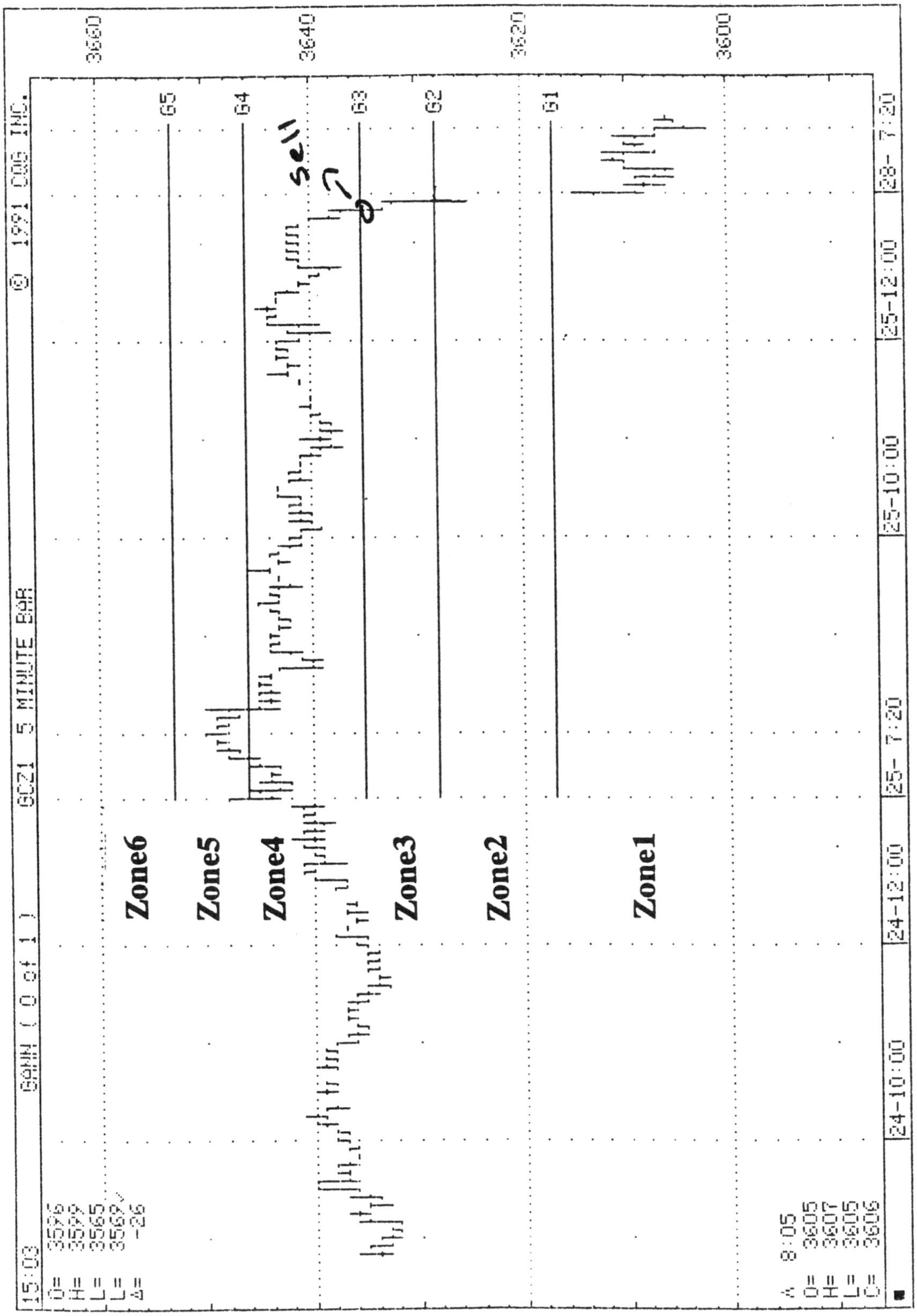
15:03
GANN (0 of 1)
GCZ1 5 MINUTE BAR
© 1991 CQG INC.
O= 3576
H= 3577
L= 3565
L= 3567
Δ= -26
3660
3640
3620
3600
65
64
63
62
61
Zone6
Zone5
Zone4
Zone3
Zone2
Zone1
sell
24-10:00
24-12:00
25- 7:20
25-10:00
25-12:00
28- 7:20
8:05
O= 3605
H= 3607
L= 3605
C= 3606

December Heating Oil (11/07)
Pattern: Zone2 Close, Zone3 Open

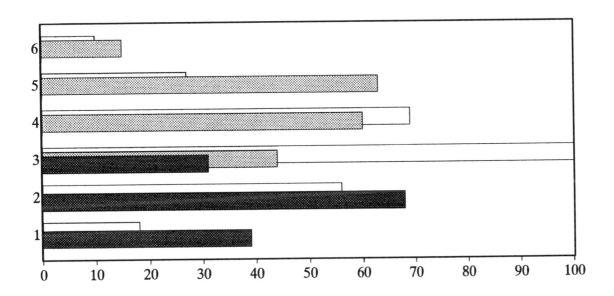

ZONE 1	ZONE 2	ZONE 3	ZONE 4	ZONE 5	ZONE 6	
		44%	60%	63%	15%	Resist.
39%	68%	31%				Support
18%	56%	100%	69%	27%	10%	Reached

Trade Analysis: Sell in Zone4 on 60% resistance or Zone5 on 63% resistance. Initiate trade on the momentum divergence. Place a stop and reverse order in Zone6 since there is only 15% resistance. Otherwise, exit in Zone2 with 68% support or on the close.

Trade Decision: Sell Zone4 on 60% resistance or Zone5 on 63% resistance and momentum divergence.

Trade Result: Sell order is placed in Zone4 at 7125. Trade is exited on the close.

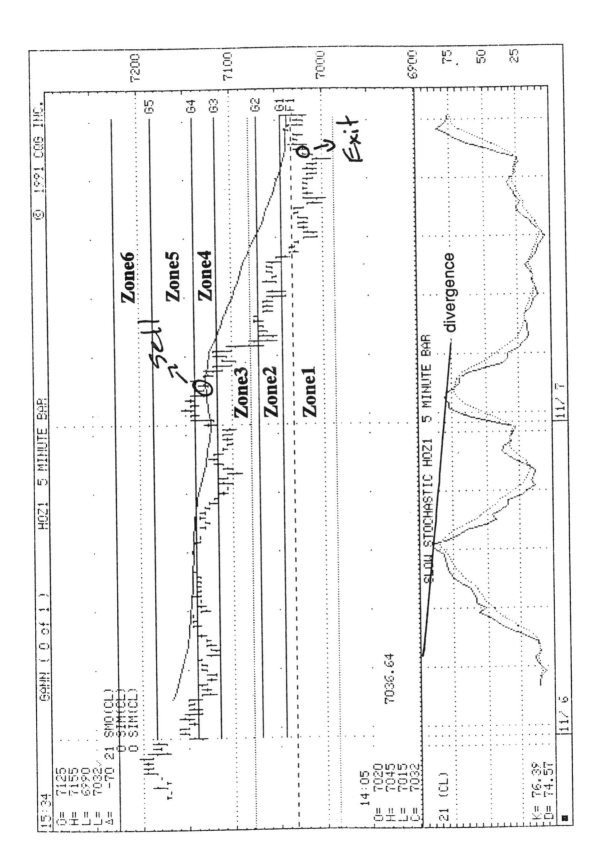

November Soybeans (10/25)
Pattern: Zone2 Close, Zone3 Open

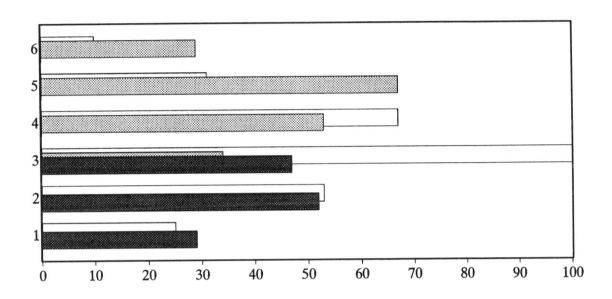

ZONE 1	ZONE 2	ZONE 3	ZONE 4	ZONE 5	ZONE 6	
		34%	53%	67%	29%	Resist.
29%	52%	47%				Support
25%	53%	100%	67%	31%	10%	Reached

Trade Analysis: Possible trades to consider are: 1) a sell stop order in Zone1 on 29% support, 2) a sell order in Zone5 on 67% resistance, 3) a buy stop order in Zone6 on 29% resistance. Since prices reach Zone1 first, the Zone1 sell stop order is filled.

Trade Decision: Sell Zone1 on 29% support on a stop order.

Trade Result: Sell stop order is placed in Zone1 at 5438. Trade is exited on the close.

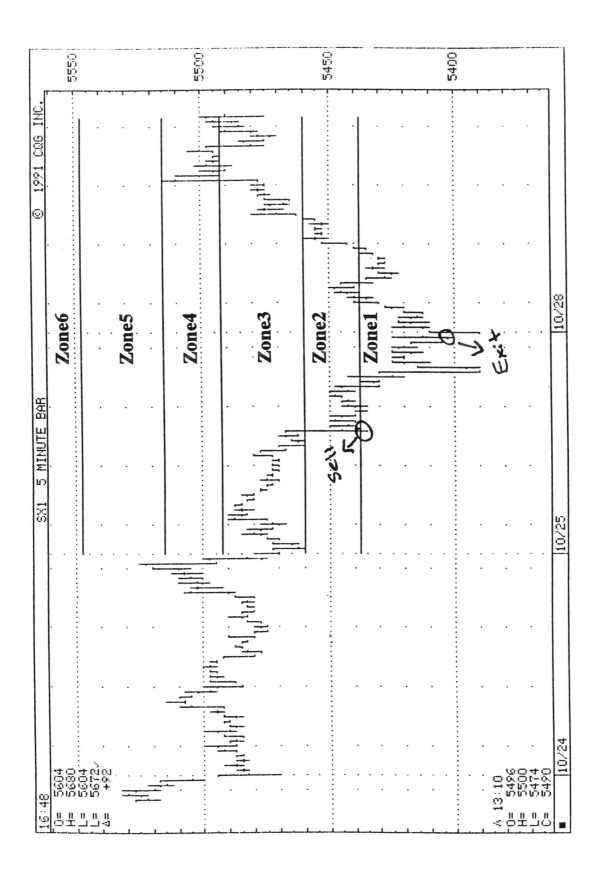

January Soybeans (11/06)
Pattern: Zone3 Close, Zone2 Open

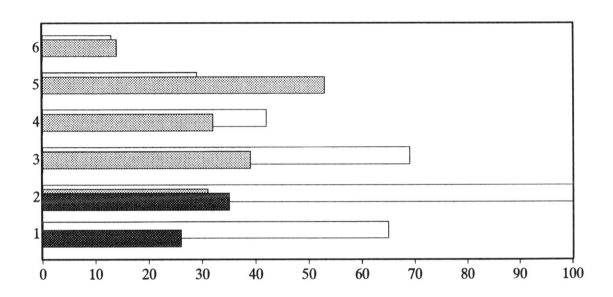

ZONE 1	ZONE 2	ZONE 3	ZONE 4	ZONE 5	ZONE 6	
	31%	39%	32%	53%	14%	Resist.
26%	35%					Support
65%	100%	69%	42%	29%	13%	Reached

Trade Analysis: Multiple low probabilities indicate a volatile day in either direction — both low support and low resistance numbers. If prices cross into Zone3 then volatility should be to the upside since Zone3 resistance is 39% and Zone4 resistance is 32%. If prices cross into Zone1, then volatility should be to the downside since Zone1 support is only 26%.

Trade Decision: Sell Zone1 on a stop order on 26% support.

Trade Result: Sell stop order is placed in Zone1 at 5645. Trade is exited on the close.

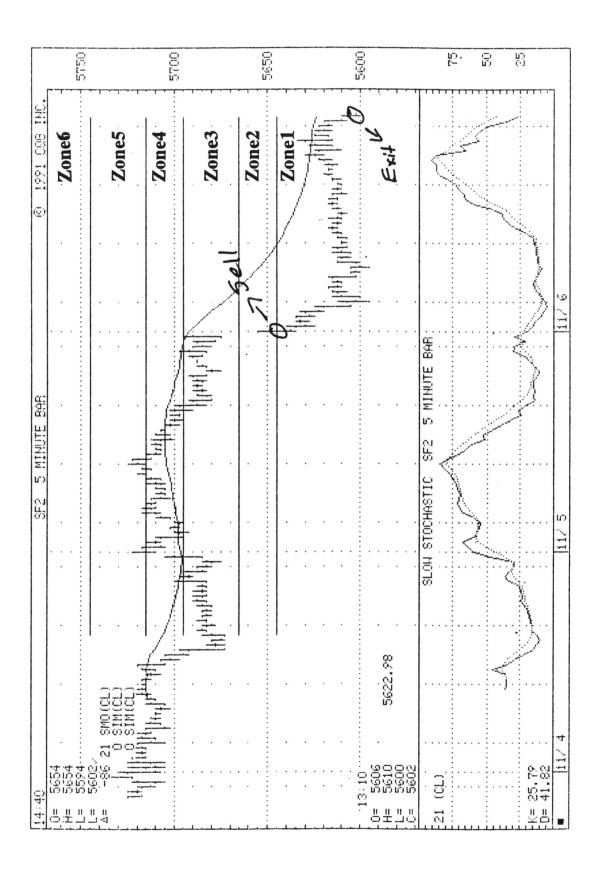

December German Mark (10/29)
Pattern: Zone1 Close, Zone4 Open

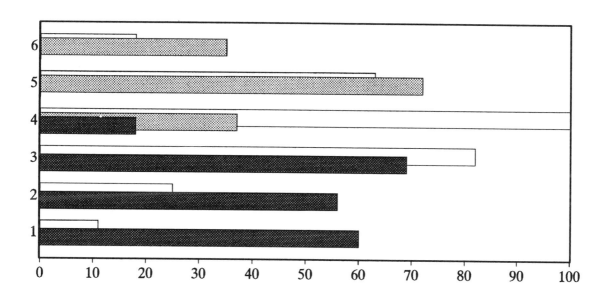

ZONE 1	ZONE 2	ZONE 3	ZONE 4	ZONE 5	ZONE 6	
		31%	37%	72%	35%	Resist.
60%	56%	69%	18%			Support
11%	25%	82%	100%	63%	18%	Reached

Trade Analysis: This trade is shown as an example of using Zone Pattern Probability Analysis combined with a long-term indicator to place a position trade with low risk. Although it is not clearly visible on this short-term graph, the 5800 level is a 38% retracement of a previous significant daily high. In addition there is a momentum divergence in Zone3 with support of 69%.

Trade Decision: Buy Zone3 on 69% support and momentum divergence. If trade is profitable at the close then hold the position.

Trade Result: Buy order is placed in Zone3 at 5801 and held for a position trade.

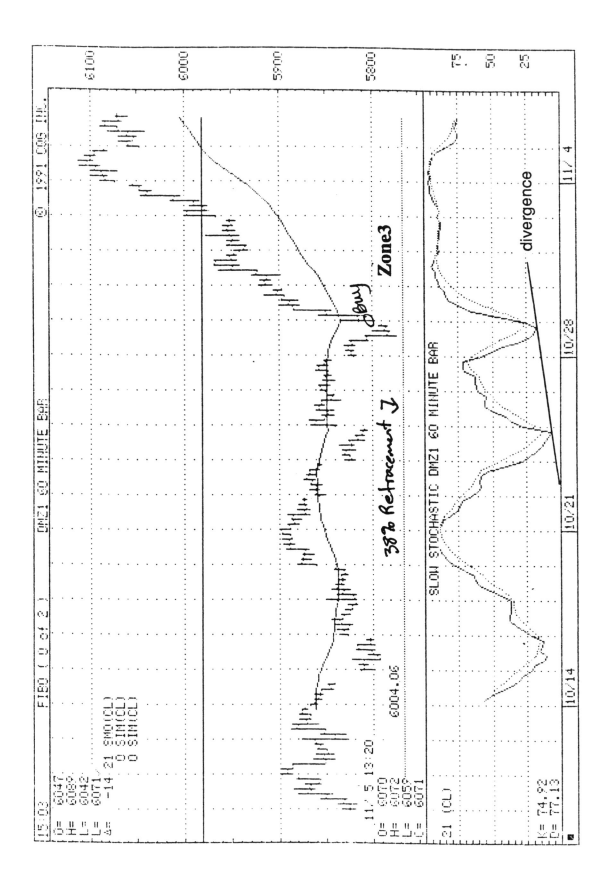

88

APPENDIX 1:

TRADING FLOWCHART

<u>Prior to Market Open:</u>

Step #1:   Compute yesterday's closing price zone
(Zones for yesterday are computed from previous day's high, low, close*)
<—1—IL2I—2—IL1I—3—IAI—4—IH1I—5—IH2I—6—>

Step #2:   Compute zones for today's open
(Zones for today are computed from yesterday's high, low, close**)
<—1—IL2I—2—IL1I—3—IAI—4—IH1I—5—IH2I—6—>

<u>After Market Open:</u>

Step #3:   Obtain the opening price zone

Step #4:   Look up the probability table for the appropriate Zone Close, Zone Open pattern

Step #5:   Determine if there are low or high zone probability percentages. If the answer is yes, then proceed to Step #6

Step #6:   Place buy orders in zones of high support or low resistance
Place sell orders in zones of high resistance or low support

* Computation for yesterday's closing zone (P = Previous day)

$A = (High(P) + Low(P) + Close (P))/3$
$L1 = (2 * A) — High(P)$
$H1 = (2 * A) — Low(P)$
$L2 = A + L1 — H1$
$H2 = A + H1 — L1$

** Computation for today's opening zone (Y = Yesterday)

$A = (High(Y) + Low(Y) + Close (Y))/3$
$L1 = (2 * A) — High(Y)$
$H1 = (2 * A) — Low(Y)$
$L2 = A + L1 — H1$
$H2 = A + H1 — L1$

APPENDIX 2:

POTENTIAL RESEARCH AREAS

After becoming accustomed to zone analysis and the probability distribution tables, it is helpful to analyze trading days according to the zones in which prices traded. This can be characterized as reading the market by zones. The zones of interest are yesterday's closing zone, today's opening zone, high zone, low zone, and closing zone. These zones can be expressed in the notation "1—3422" where:

---

1 = yesterday's closing zone
3 = today's opening zone
4 = today's high zone
2 = today's low zone
2 = today's closing zone

The graph on the follow page shows June 1991 Treasury Bonds with some zone price patterns marked. Classifying trading days according to zone patterns provides a unique method to visualize and analyze how prices traded. By labeling these zone classifications on a bar graph, you can look for a correlation between zone patterns and specific types of price action such as volatility. Notice January 18th, January 30th, February 12th, and April 16th. Each of these days had a Zone5 closing pattern, i.e., the preceding day closed in Zone5. Zone5 closes are intriguing because prices did not have enough momentum to rally strongly and close in Zone6. It is often the case, especially in a weak market, that prices will rally slightly the next day, and then close hard down. Notice on the days following the Zone5 closes, that prices were able to rally one zone above the opening zone, and then prices closed down significantly.

This pattern, as well as others, might be applied to predict volatile price movement. Currently, I have not performed extensive research in this area. If you enjoy research in the futures market, this may be an interesting and fruitful avenue to pursue. Many daytrading systems are based purely on determining volatility and breakout prices. Zone Pattern Probabilities provide both a method for classifying days preceding volatility, as well as a method for determining a strategic place to enter a trade.

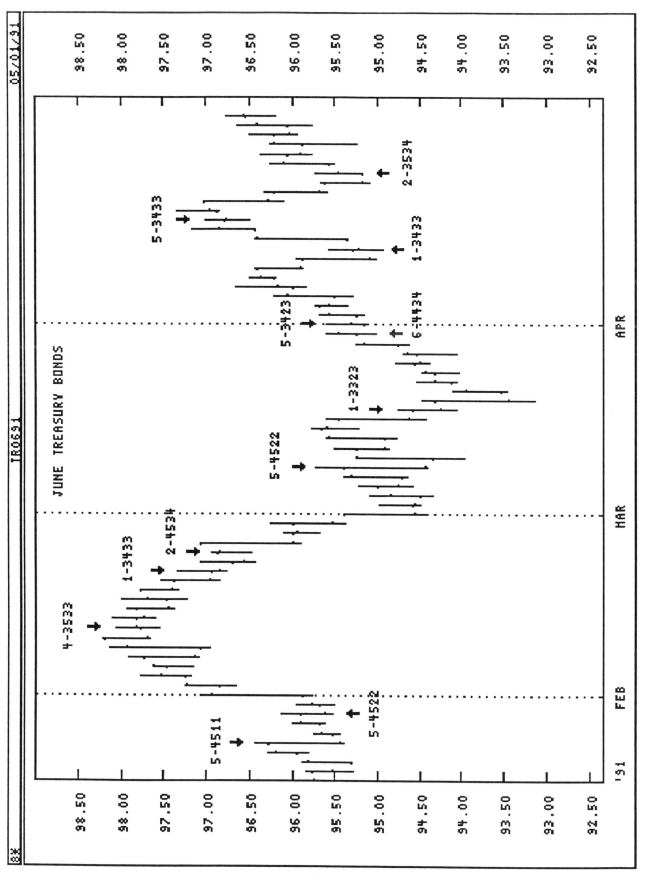

JUNE TREASURY BONDS

APPENDIX 3:

PROBABILITY DISTRIBUTION TABLES

Z O N E S (1) - (6)   : ZONE(?) CLOSE, ZONE(?) OPEN

(1)	(2)	(3)	(4)	(5)	(6)	:	
						:	Zone(1) Close, Zone(1) Open
50%	0%	0%	0%	100%		:	Zone Resistance
50%						:	Zone Support
100%	50%	50%	50%	50%	0%	:	Zone Reached
						:	Zone(1) Close, Zone(2) Open
	33%	50%	67%	0%	0%	:	Zone Resistance
20%	44%					:	Zone Support
56%	100%	67%	33%	11%	11%	:	Zone Reached
						:	Zone(1) Close, Zone(3) Open
		46%	70%	84%	0%	:	Zone Resistance
49%	62%	52%				:	Zone Support
18%	48%	100%	54%	16%	3%	:	Zone Reached
						:	Zone(1) Close, Zone(4) Open
			62%	55%	20%	:	Zone Resistance
0%	80%	52%	28%			:	Zone Support
7%	34%	72%	100%	38%	17%	:	Zone Reached
						:	Zone(1) Close, Zone(5) Open
			80%	0%		:	Zone Resistance
		100%	33%	40%		:	Zone Support
0%	0%	40%	60%	100%	20%	:	Zone Reached
						:	Zone(1) Close, Zone(6) Open
				50%		:	Zone Resistance
0%	0%	0%	0%	50%	0%	:	Zone Support
50%	50%	50%	50%	100%	100%	:	Zone Reached
						:	Zone(2) Close, Zone(1) Open
25%	67%	100%				:	Zone Resistance
50%						:	Zone Support
100%	75%	25%	0%	0%	0%	:	Zone Reached
						:	Zone(2) Close, Zone(2) Open
	11%	56%	43%	25%	33%	:	Zone Resistance
11%	50%					:	Zone Support
50%	100%	89%	39%	22%	17%	:	Zone Reached
						:	Zone(2) Close, Zone(3) Open
		35%	64%	71%	25%	:	Zone Resistance
34%	59%	52%				:	Zone Support
20%	48%	100%	66%	23%	7%	:	Zone Reached
						:	Zone(2) Close, Zone(4) Open
			40%	48%	38%	:	Zone Resistance
25%	67%	67%	31%			:	Zone Support
8%	23%	69%	100%	60%	31%	:	Zone Reached
						:	Zone(2) Close, Zone(5) Open
			33%	50%		:	Zone Resistance
100%	0%	50%	33%	0%		:	Zone Support
33%	33%	67%	100%	100%	67%	:	Zone Reached
						:	Zone(2) Close, Zone(6) Open
					0%	:	Zone Resistance
					100%	:	Zone Support
0%	0%	0%	0%	0%	100%	:	Zone Reached
						:	Zone(3) Close, Zone(1) Open
25%	22%	14%	0%	50%	33%	:	Zone Resistance
50%						:	Zone Support
100%	75%	58%	50%	50%	25%	:	Zone Reached
						:	Zone(3) Close, Zone(2) Open
	10%	59%	27%	50%	75%	:	Zone Resistance
50%	27%					:	Zone Support
73%	100%	90%	37%	27%	13%	:	Zone Reached
						:	Zone(3) Close, Zone(3) Open
		21%	50%	61%	49%	:	Zone Resistance
45%	47%	48%				:	Zone Support
27%	52%	100%	79%	39%	15%	:	Zone Reached
						:	Zone(3) Close, Zone(4) Open
			35%	54%	32%	:	Zone Resistance
50%	56%	53%	33%			:	Zone Support
14%	31%	67%	100%	65%	30%	:	Zone Reached
						:	Zone(3) Close, Zone(5) Open
			26%	59%		:	Zone Resistance
29%	12%	27%	39%	22%		:	Zone Support
30%	35%	48%	78%	100%	74%	:	Zone Reached
						:	Zone(3) Close, Zone(6) Open
					67%	:	Zone Resistance
			100%	67%	0%	:	Zone Support
0%	0%	0%	33%	100%	100%	:	Zone Reached

ZONES (1) - (6)   : ZONE(?) CLOSE, ZONE(?) OPEN

(1)	(2)	(3)	(4)	(5)	(6)	Description
						: Zone(4) Close, Zone(1) Open
40%	44%	20%	75%	0%	0%	Zone Resistance
60%						Zone Support
100%	60%	33%	27%	7%	7%	Zone Reached
						: Zone(4) Close, Zone(2) Open
	14%	48%	31%	56%	50%	Zone Resistance
61%	38%					Zone Support
62%	100%	86%	45%	31%	14%	Zone Reached
						: Zone(4) Close, Zone(3) Open
		23%	55%	59%	32%	Zone Resistance
49%	49%	36%				Zone Support
32%	64%	100%	78%	34%	14%	Zone Reached
						: Zone(4) Close, Zone(4) Open
			39%	50%	39%	Zone Resistance
47%	58%	52%	28%			Zone Support
15%	35%	72%	100%	61%	30%	Zone Reached
						: Zone(4) Close, Zone(5) Open
				30%	38%	Zone Resistance
100%	62%	47%	44%	27%		Zone Support
8%	22%	41%	73%	100%	70%	Zone Reached
						: Zone(4) Close, Zone(6) Open
					62%	Zone Resistance
33%	40%	0%	17%	33%	31%	Zone Support
23%	38%	38%	46%	69%	100%	Zone Reached
						: Zone(5) Close, Zone(1) Open
0%	0%	50%	0%	0%	100%	Zone Resistance
50%						Zone Support
100%	100%	100%	50%	50%	50%	Zone Reached
						: Zone(5) Close, Zone(2) Open
	20%	25%	100%			Zone Resistance
0%	60%					Zone Support
40%	100%	80%	60%	0%	0%	Zone Reached
						: Zone(5) Close, Zone(3) Open
		14%	74%	60%	50%	Zone Resistance
36%	59%	39%				Zone Support
25%	61%	100%	86%	23%	9%	Zone Reached
						: Zone(5) Close, Zone(4) Open
			54%	64%	32%	Zone Resistance
42%	77%	62%	29%			Zone Support
6%	27%	71%	100%	46%	16%	Zone Reached
						: Zone(5) Close, Zone(5) Open
			38%	0%		Zone Resistance
100%	0%	50%	50%	50%		Zone Support
12%	12%	25%	50%	100%	62%	Zone Reached
						: Zone(5) Close, Zone(6) Open
					0%	Zone Resistance
				100%	80%	Zone Support
0%	0%	0%	0%	20%	100%	Zone Reached
						: Zone(6) Close, Zone(1) Open
100%						Zone Resistance
0%						Zone Support
100%	0%	0%	0%	0%	0%	Zone Reached
						: Zone(6) Close, Zone(2) Open
	67%	0%	0%	0%	100%	Zone Resistance
50%	33%					Zone Support
67%	100%	33%	33%	33%	33%	Zone Reached
						: Zone(6) Close, Zone(3) Open
		11%	82%	67%	100%	Zone Resistance
50%	80%	47%				Zone Support
11%	53%	100%	89%	16%	5%	Zone Reached
						: Zone(6) Close, Zone(4) Open
			58%	62%	57%	Zone Resistance
67%	76%	72%	45%			Zone Support
4%	16%	55%	100%	42%	16%	Zone Reached
						: Zone(6) Close, Zone(5) Open
				42%	43%	Zone Resistance
50%	0%	67%	45%	8%		Zone Support
17%	17%	50%	92%	100%	58%	Zone Reached
						: Zone(6) Close, Zone(6) Open
					67%	Zone Resistance
			100%	50%	33%	Zone Support
0%	0%	0%	33%	67%	100%	Zone Reached

```
Z O N E S   (1) - (6)            : ZONE(?) CLOSE, ZONE(?) OPEN


      (1)    (2)    (3)    (4)    (5)    (6)
  ------------------------------------------- : Zone(1) Close, Zone(1) Open
      27%    50%    50%    50%     0%   100%  :    Zone Resistance
      45%                                     :    Zone Support
     100%    73%    36%    18%     9%     9%  :    Zone Reached
  ------------------------------------------- : Zone(1) Close, Zone(2) Open
             17%    50%    42%    71%   100%  :    Zone Resistance
      56%    45%                              :    Zone Support
      55%   100%    83%    41%    24%     7%  :    Zone Reached
  ------------------------------------------- : Zone(1) Close, Zone(3) Open
                    43%    69%    73%    33%  :    Zone Resistance
      64%    72%    52%                       :    Zone Support
      13%    48%   100%    57%    18%     5%  :    Zone Reached
  ------------------------------------------- : Zone(1) Close, Zone(4) Open
                           52%    75%    60%  :    Zone Resistance
      80%    62%    62%    19%                :    Zone Support
      12%    31%    81%   100%    48%    12%  :    Zone Reached
  ------------------------------------------- : Zone(1) Close, Zone(5) Open
                                  50%    29%  :    Zone Resistance
       0%     0%    71%    22%    36%         :    Zone Support
      14%    14%    50%    64%   100%    50%  :    Zone Reached
  ------------------------------------------- : Zone(1) Close, Zone(6) Open
                                         0%   :    Zone Resistance
                                 100%    0%   :    Zone Support
       0%     0%     0%     0%   100%   100%  :    Zone Reached
  ------------------------------------------- : Zone(2) Close, Zone(1) Open
      25%    67%    67%   100%                :    Zone Resistance
      75%                                     :    Zone Support
     100%    75%    25%     8%     0%     0%  :    Zone Reached
  ------------------------------------------- : Zone(2) Close, Zone(2) Open
             29%    52%    42%    71%    50%  :    Zone Resistance
      61%    34%                              :    Zone Support
      66%   100%    71%    34%    20%     6%  :    Zone Reached
  ------------------------------------------- : Zone(2) Close, Zone(3) Open
                    35%    60%    72%    50%  :    Zone Resistance
      36%    57%    43%                       :    Zone Support
      24%    57%   100%    65%    26%     7%  :    Zone Reached
  ------------------------------------------- : Zone(2) Close, Zone(4) Open
                           31%    59%    47%  :    Zone Resistance
      29%    50%    68%    34%                :    Zone Support
      10%    21%    66%   100%    69%    28%  :    Zone Reached
  ------------------------------------------- : Zone(2) Close, Zone(5) Open
                                  33%    62%  :    Zone Resistance
     100%    50%    67%    40%    17%         :    Zone Support
       8%    17%    50%    83%   100%    67%  :    Zone Reached
  ------------------------------------------- : Zone(2) Close, Zone(6) Open
                                         33%  :    Zone Resistance
                                 100%    33%  :    Zone Support
       0%     0%     0%     0%    67%   100%  :    Zone Reached
  ------------------------------------------- : Zone(3) Close, Zone(1) Open
      33%    64%    40%    33%    50%     0%  :    Zone Resistance
      33%                                     :    Zone Support
     100%    67%    24%    14%    10%     5%  :    Zone Reached
  ------------------------------------------- : Zone(3) Close, Zone(2) Open
             27%    47%    43%    38%    38%  :    Zone Resistance
      49%    34%                              :    Zone Support
      66%   100%    73%    39%    22%    14%  :    Zone Reached
  ------------------------------------------- : Zone(3) Close, Zone(3) Open
                    29%    55%    70%    43%  :    Zone Resistance
      48%    55%    39%                       :    Zone Support
      27%    61%   100%    71%    32%    10%  :    Zone Reached
  ------------------------------------------- : Zone(3) Close, Zone(4) Open
                           33%    54%    52%  :    Zone Resistance
      42%    61%    56%    29%                :    Zone Support
      12%    31%    71%   100%    67%    31%  :    Zone Reached
  ------------------------------------------- : Zone(3) Close, Zone(5) Open
                                  28%    38%  :    Zone Resistance
       0%    75%    69%    61%    30%         :    Zone Support
       2%     9%    28%    70%   100%    72%  :    Zone Reached
  ------------------------------------------- : Zone(3) Close, Zone(6) Open
                                         40%  :    Zone Resistance
     100%    67%    25%    43%    53%    40%  :    Zone Support
       4%    12%    16%    28%    60%   100%  :    Zone Reached
```

ZONES (1) - (6)   : ZONE(?) CLOSE, ZONE(?) OPEN

(1)	(2)	(3)	(4)	(5)	(6)	Metric
						Zone(4) Close, Zone(1) Open
57%	67%	67%	0%	0%	100%	Zone Resistance
29%						Zone Support
100%	43%	14%	5%	5%	5%	Zone Reached
						Zone(4) Close, Zone(2) Open
	19%	46%	53%	67%	33%	Zone Resistance
50%	49%					Zone Support
51%	100%	81%	44%	21%	7%	Zone Reached
						Zone(4) Close, Zone(3) Open
		24%	44%	67%	44%	Zone Resistance
46%	52%	39%				Zone Support
29%	61%	100%	76%	42%	14%	Zone Reached
						Zone(4) Close, Zone(4) Open
			34%	53%	37%	Zone Resistance
39%	61%	49%	33%			Zone Support
13%	34%	67%	100%	66%	31%	Zone Reached
						Zone(4) Close, Zone(5) Open
				44%	60%	Zone Resistance
14%	46%	50%	47%	21%		Zone Support
11%	21%	42%	79%	100%	56%	Zone Reached
						Zone(4) Close, Zone(6) Open
					42%	Zone Resistance
0%	50%	33%	45%	42%	39%	Zone Support
6%	13%	19%	35%	61%	100%	Zone Reached
						Zone(5) Close, Zone(1) Open
33%	50%	100%				Zone Resistance
33%						Zone Support
100%	67%	33%	0%	0%	0%	Zone Reached
						Zone(5) Close, Zone(2) Open
	24%	62%	80%	0%	100%	Zone Resistance
36%	35%					Zone Support
65%	100%	76%	29%	6%	6%	Zone Reached
						Zone(5) Close, Zone(3) Open
		26%	71%	43%	50%	Zone Resistance
24%	51%	34%				Zone Support
32%	66%	100%	74%	22%	12%	Zone Reached
						Zone(5) Close, Zone(4) Open
			46%	58%	44%	Zone Resistance
42%	56%	49%	37%			Zone Support
14%	32%	63%	100%	54%	23%	Zone Reached
						Zone(5) Close, Zone(5) Open
				37%	41%	Zone Resistance
40%	17%	45%	59%	23%		Zone Support
14%	17%	31%	77%	100%	63%	Zone Reached
						Zone(5) Close, Zone(6) Open
					63%	Zone Resistance
	100%	60%	55%	35%	11%	Zone Support
0%	11%	26%	58%	89%	100%	Zone Reached
						Zone(6) Close, Zone(1) Open
100%						Zone Resistance
0%						Zone Support
100%	0%	0%	0%	0%	0%	Zone Reached
						Zone(6) Close, Zone(2) Open
	21%	64%	50%	0%	50%	Zone Resistance
0%	50%					Zone Support
50%	100%	79%	29%	14%	14%	Zone Reached
						Zone(6) Close, Zone(3) Open
		23%	65%	64%	40%	Zone Resistance
57%	76%	44%				Zone Support
13%	56%	100%	77%	27%	10%	Zone Reached
						Zone(6) Close, Zone(4) Open
			49%	65%	38%	Zone Resistance
50%	76%	74%	47%			Zone Support
3%	14%	53%	100%	51%	18%	Zone Reached
						Zone(6) Close, Zone(5) Open
				31%	37%	Zone Resistance
0%	60%	17%	79%	28%		Zone Support
5%	13%	15%	72%	100%	69%	Zone Reached
						Zone(6) Close, Zone(6) Open
					70%	Zone Resistance
50%	0%	33%	75%	20%	25%	Zone Support
10%	10%	15%	60%	75%	100%	Zone Reached

Z O N E S (1) - (6)   : ZONE(?) CLOSE, ZONE(?) OPEN

(1)	(2)	(3)	(4)	(5)	(6)		
						:	Zone(1) Close, Zone(1) Open
29%	60%	50%	100%			:	Zone Resistance
29%						:	Zone Support
100%	71%	29%	14%	0%	0%	:	Zone Reached
						:	Zone(1) Close, Zone(2) Open
	7%	58%	45%	83%	0%	:	Zone Resistance
82%	61%					:	Zone Support
39%	100%	93%	39%	21%	4%	:	Zone Reached
						:	Zone(1) Close, Zone(3) Open
		47%	72%	70%	62%	:	Zone Resistance
53%	63%	51%				:	Zone Support
18%	49%	100%	53%	15%	4%	:	Zone Reached
						:	Zone(1) Close, Zone(4) Open
			36%	65%	62%	:	Zone Resistance
0%	80%	63%	25%			:	Zone Support
6%	28%	75%	100%	64%	22%	:	Zone Reached
						:	Zone(1) Close, Zone(5) Open
				60%	25%	:	Zone Resistance
100%	0%	67%	62%	20%		:	Zone Support
10%	10%	30%	80%	100%	40%	:	Zone Reached
						:	Zone(1) Close, Zone(6) Open
					50%	:	Zone Resistance
	100%	0%	0%	0%	50%	:	Zone Support
0%	50%	50%	50%	50%	100%	:	Zone Reached
						:	Zone(2) Close, Zone(1) Open
30%	36%	78%	0%	100%		:	Zone Resistance
55%						:	Zone Support
100%	70%	45%	10%	10%	0%	:	Zone Reached
						:	Zone(2) Close, Zone(2) Open
	13%	35%	62%	80%	100%	:	Zone Resistance
54%	43%					:	Zone Support
57%	100%	87%	57%	22%	4%	:	Zone Reached
						:	Zone(2) Close, Zone(3) Open
		23%	56%	69%	53%	:	Zone Resistance
56%	56%	50%				:	Zone Support
22%	50%	100%	77%	34%	10%	:	Zone Reached
						:	Zone(2) Close, Zone(4) Open
			36%	61%	21%	:	Zone Resistance
0%	64%	69%	36%			:	Zone Support
7%	20%	64%	100%	64%	25%	:	Zone Reached
						:	Zone(2) Close, Zone(5) Open
				38%	50%	:	Zone Resistance
0%	50%	71%	22%	31%		:	Zone Support
8%	15%	54%	69%	100%	62%	:	Zone Reached
						:	Zone(2) Close, Zone(6) Open
					50%	:	Zone Resistance
			100%	0%	75%	:	Zone Support
0%	0%	0%	25%	25%	100%	:	Zone Reached
						:	Zone(3) Close, Zone(1) Open
57%	40%	33%	50%	50%	100%	:	Zone Resistance
26%						:	Zone Support
100%	43%	26%	17%	9%	4%	:	Zone Reached
						:	Zone(3) Close, Zone(2) Open
	23%	35%	54%	58%	40%	:	Zone Resistance
48%	37%					:	Zone Support
63%	100%	77%	50%	23%	10%	:	Zone Reached
						:	Zone(3) Close, Zone(3) Open
		32%	49%	69%	55%	:	Zone Resistance
52%	50%	38%				:	Zone Support
31%	62%	100%	69%	35%	11%	:	Zone Reached
						:	Zone(3) Close, Zone(4) Open
			33%	50%	53%	:	Zone Resistance
47%	62%	62%	32%			:	Zone Support
10%	26%	68%	100%	67%	34%	:	Zone Reached
						:	Zone(3) Close, Zone(5) Open
				30%	61%	:	Zone Resistance
100%	86%	53%	55%	18%		:	Zone Support
2%	18%	38%	82%	100%	70%	:	Zone Reached
						:	Zone(3) Close, Zone(6) Open
					30%	:	Zone Resistance
50%	0%	33%	57%	53%	25%	:	Zone Support
10%	10%	15%	35%	75%	100%	:	Zone Reached

Z O N E S (1) - (6)   : ZONE(?) CLOSE, ZONE(?) OPEN

(1)	(2)	(3)	(4)	(5)	(6)		
						:	Zone(4) Close, Zone(1) Open
45%	45%	83%	0%	0%	0%	:	Zone Resistance
55%						:	Zone Support
100%	55%	30%	5%	5%	5%	:	Zone Reached
						:	Zone(4) Close, Zone(2) Open
	22%	34%	64%	67%	67%	:	Zone Resistance
56%	45%					:	Zone Support
55%	100%	78%	51%	18%	6%	:	Zone Reached
						:	Zone(4) Close, Zone(3) Open
		24%	41%	61%	40%	:	Zone Resistance
45%	51%	44%				:	Zone Support
27%	56%	100%	76%	45%	17%	:	Zone Reached
						:	Zone(4) Close, Zone(4) Open
			39%	58%	37%	:	Zone Resistance
34%	52%	55%	37%			:	Zone Support
14%	29%	63%	100%	61%	26%	:	Zone Reached
						:	Zone(4) Close, Zone(5) Open
				31%	60%	:	Zone Resistance
57%	46%	38%	60%	13%		:	Zone Support
11%	21%	34%	87%	100%	69%	:	Zone Reached
						:	Zone(4) Close, Zone(6) Open
					57%	:	Zone Resistance
	100%	33%	0%	60%	35%	:	Zone Support
0%	17%	26%	26%	65%	100%	:	Zone Reached
						:	Zone(5) Close, Zone(1) Open
25%	33%	100%				:	Zone Resistance
75%						:	Zone Support
100%	75%	50%	0%	0%	0%	:	Zone Reached
						:	Zone(5) Close, Zone(2) Open
	27%	64%	50%	100%		:	Zone Resistance
18%	27%					:	Zone Support
73%	100%	73%	27%	13%	0%	:	Zone Reached
						:	Zone(5) Close, Zone(3) Open
		34%	68%	60%	25%	:	Zone Resistance
40%	67%	40%				:	Zone Support
20%	60%	100%	68%	20%	8%	:	Zone Reached
						:	Zone(5) Close, Zone(4) Open
			51%	42%	46%	:	Zone Resistance
38%	67%	52%	37%			:	Zone Support
10%	30%	63%	100%	49%	29%	:	Zone Reached
						:	Zone(5) Close, Zone(5) Open
				33%	41%	:	Zone Resistance
75%	0%	50%	69%	21%		:	Zone Support
12%	12%	24%	79%	100%	67%	:	Zone Reached
						:	Zone(5) Close, Zone(6) Open
					48%	:	Zone Resistance
0%	67%	25%	43%	53%	40%	:	Zone Support
4%	12%	16%	28%	60%	100%	:	Zone Reached
						:	Zone(6) Close, Zone(1) Open
100%						:	Zone Resistance
0%						:	Zone Support
100%	0%	0%	0%	0%	0%	:	Zone Reached
						:	Zone(6) Close, Zone(2) Open
	36%	43%	50%	0%	50%	:	Zone Resistance
0%	55%					:	Zone Support
45%	100%	64%	36%	18%	18%	:	Zone Reached
						:	Zone(6) Close, Zone(3) Open
		20%	64%	56%	86%	:	Zone Resistance
43%	76%	48%				:	Zone Support
12%	52%	100%	80%	29%	12%	:	Zone Reached
						:	Zone(6) Close, Zone(4) Open
			46%	69%	37%	:	Zone Resistance
67%	77%	72%	47%			:	Zone Support
3%	15%	53%	100%	54%	17%	:	Zone Reached
						:	Zone(6) Close, Zone(5) Open
				29%	59%	:	Zone Resistance
0%	0%	40%	74%	21%		:	Zone Support
12%	12%	21%	79%	100%	71%	:	Zone Reached
						:	Zone(6) Close, Zone(6) Open
					74%	:	Zone Resistance
0%	50%	50%	60%	23%	32%	:	Zone Support
5%	11%	21%	53%	68%	100%	:	Zone Reached

ZONES (1) - (6)   : ZONE(?) CLOSE, ZONE(?) OPEN

	(1)	(2)	(3)	(4)	(5)	(6)	:	
							:	Zone(1) Close, Zone(1) Open
	41%	65%	62%	67%	100%		:	Zone Resistance
	51%						:	Zone Support
	100%	59%	21%	8%	3%	0%	:	Zone Reached
							:	Zone(1) Close, Zone(2) Open
		12%	69%	47%	38%	60%	:	Zone Resistance
	47%	43%					:	Zone Support
	57%	100%	88%	27%	14%	9%	:	Zone Reached
							:	Zone(1) Close, Zone(3) Open
			38%	63%	71%	46%	:	Zone Resistance
	40%	60%	51%				:	Zone Support
	20%	49%	100%	62%	22%	6%	:	Zone Reached
							:	Zone(1) Close, Zone(4) Open
				37%	71%	47%	:	Zone Resistance
	40%	71%	76%	20%			:	Zone Support
	5%	19%	79%	99%	64%	19%	:	Zone Reached
							:	Zone(1) Close, Zone(5) Open
					40%	62%	:	Zone Resistance
		100%	54%	62%	21%		:	Zone Support
	0%	14%	30%	79%	100%	60%	:	Zone Reached
							:	Zone(1) Close, Zone(6) Open
						37%	:	Zone Resistance
			100%	40%	44%	53%	:	Zone Support
	0%	0%	16%	26%	47%	100%	:	Zone Reached
							:	Zone(2) Close, Zone(1) Open
	40%	50%	29%	27%	43%	75%	:	Zone Resistance
	53%						:	Zone Support
	100%	60%	30%	23%	15%	9%	:	Zone Reached
							:	Zone(2) Close, Zone(2) Open
		16%	58%	50%	70%	0%	:	Zone Resistance
	49%	32%					:	Zone Support
	68%	100%	84%	35%	18%	5%	:	Zone Reached
							:	Zone(2) Close, Zone(3) Open
			25%	64%	82%	29%	:	Zone Resistance
	53%	59%	46%				:	Zone Support
	22%	54%	100%	75%	27%	5%	:	Zone Reached
							:	Zone(2) Close, Zone(4) Open
				34%	63%	40%	:	Zone Resistance
	50%	83%	76%	19%			:	Zone Support
	3%	19%	81%	100%	66%	24%	:	Zone Reached
							:	Zone(2) Close, Zone(5) Open
					29%	60%	:	Zone Resistance
	0%	33%	67%	61%	34%		:	Zone Support
	6%	9%	26%	66%	100%	71%	:	Zone Reached
							:	Zone(2) Close, Zone(6) Open
						45%	:	Zone Resistance
			100%	67%	79%	30%	:	Zone Support
	0%	0%	5%	15%	70%	100%	:	Zone Reached
							:	Zone(3) Close, Zone(1) Open
	53%	64%	70%	0%	33%	50%	:	Zone Resistance
	35%						:	Zone Support
	100%	47%	17%	5%	5%	3%	:	Zone Reached
							:	Zone(3) Close, Zone(2) Open
		24%	61%	38%	44%	56%	:	Zone Resistance
	41%	32%					:	Zone Support
	68%	100%	76%	30%	18%	10%	:	Zone Reached
							:	Zone(3) Close, Zone(3) Open
			24%	58%	59%	52%	:	Zone Resistance
	41%	59%	41%				:	Zone Support
	24%	59%	100%	77%	31%	13%	:	Zone Reached
							:	Zone(3) Close, Zone(4) Open
				37%	65%	40%	:	Zone Resistance
	40%	53%	61%	29%			:	Zone Support
	13%	28%	71%	100%	63%	22%	:	Zone Reached
							:	Zone(3) Close, Zone(5) Open
					37%	53%	:	Zone Resistance
	33%	62%	62%	58%	30%		:	Zone Support
	4%	11%	30%	70%	100%	63%	:	Zone Reached
							:	Zone(3) Close, Zone(6) Open
						52%	:	Zone Resistance
	0%	33%	62%	56%	47%	37%	:	Zone Support
	4%	6%	15%	33%	63%	100%	:	Zone Reached

*** SWISS ***

Z O N E S (1) - (6)   : ZONE(?) CLOSE, ZONE(?) OPEN

(1)	(2)	(3)	(4)	(5)	(6)		
						:	Zone(4) Close, Zone(1) Open
40%	61%	25%	78%	50%	100%	:	Zone Resistance
50%						:	Zone Support
100%	60%	23%	17%	4%	2%	:	Zone Reached
						:	Zone(4) Close, Zone(2) Open
	27%	61%	78%	25%	67%	:	Zone Resistance
38%	35%					:	Zone Support
65%	100%	73%	30%	5%	4%	:	Zone Reached
						:	Zone(4) Close, Zone(3) Open
		29%	56%	60%	24%	:	Zone Resistance
58%	60%	35%				:	Zone Support
26%	65%	100%	72%	30%	12%	:	Zone Reached
						:	Zone(4) Close, Zone(4) Open
			48%	42%	42%	:	Zone Resistance
58%	59%	50%	32%			:	Zone Support
14%	34%	68%	100%	52%	31%	:	Zone Reached
						:	Zone(4) Close, Zone(5) Open
				26%	52%	:	Zone Resistance
33%	25%	84%	57%	26%		:	Zone Support
4%	5%	32%	74%	100%	74%	:	Zone Reached
						:	Zone(4) Close, Zone(6) Open
					36%	:	Zone Resistance
0%	0%	50%	75%	67%	47%	:	Zone Support
2%	2%	4%	18%	53%	100%	:	Zone Reached
						:	Zone(5) Close, Zone(1) Open
41%	70%	67%	0%	0%	100%	:	Zone Resistance
24%						:	Zone Support
100%	59%	18%	6%	6%	6%	:	Zone Reached
						:	Zone(5) Close, Zone(2) Open
	23%	56%	67%	25%	33%	:	Zone Resistance
57%	34%					:	Zone Support
66%	100%	77%	34%	11%	9%	:	Zone Reached
						:	Zone(5) Close, Zone(3) Open
		29%	62%	67%	62%	:	Zone Resistance
43%	66%	31%				:	Zone Support
24%	69%	100%	71%	27%	9%	:	Zone Reached
						:	Zone(5) Close, Zone(4) Open
			54%	46%	58%	:	Zone Resistance
45%	66%	50%	38%			:	Zone Support
11%	31%	62%	100%	46%	25%	:	Zone Reached
						:	Zone(5) Close, Zone(5) Open
				43%	59%	:	Zone Resistance
100%	50%	75%	53%	28%		:	Zone Support
4%	9%	34%	72%	100%	57%	:	Zone Reached
						:	Zone(5) Close, Zone(6) Open
					36%	:	Zone Resistance
	100%	50%	60%	67%	46%	:	Zone Support
0%	4%	7%	18%	54%	100%	:	Zone Reached
						:	Zone(6) Close, Zone(1) Open
50%	55%	40%	33%	50%	100%	:	Zone Resistance
41%						:	Zone Support
100%	50%	23%	14%	9%	5%	:	Zone Reached
						:	Zone(6) Close, Zone(2) Open
	23%	58%	70%	0%	33%	:	Zone Resistance
58%	61%					:	Zone Support
39%	100%	77%	32%	10%	10%	:	Zone Reached
						:	Zone(6) Close, Zone(3) Open
		16%	74%	56%	38%	:	Zone Resistance
78%	79%	47%				:	Zone Support
11%	53%	100%	84%	22%	10%	:	Zone Reached
						:	Zone(6) Close, Zone(4) Open
			50%	59%	65%	:	Zone Resistance
0%	83%	59%	44%			:	Zone Support
4%	23%	56%	100%	50%	21%	:	Zone Reached
						:	Zone(6) Close, Zone(5) Open
				42%	68%	:	Zone Resistance
40%	38%	53%	50%	11%		:	Zone Support
13%	21%	45%	89%	100%	58%	:	Zone Reached
						:	Zone(6) Close, Zone(6) Open
					60%	:	Zone Resistance
	100%	50%	54%	48%	29%	:	Zone Support
0%	9%	17%	37%	71%	100%	:	Zone Reached

ZONES (1) - (6)   : ZONE(?) CLOSE, ZONE(?) OPEN

(1)	(2)	(3)	(4)	(5)	(6)	:	
						:	Zone(1) Close, Zone(1) Open
38%	37%	62%	67%	67%	0%	:	Zone Resistance
54%						:	Zone Support
100%	62%	39%	15%	5%	2%	:	Zone Reached
						:	Zone(1) Close, Zone(2) Open
	18%	70%	41%	44%	20%	:	Zone Resistance
46%	43%					:	Zone Support
57%	100%	82%	26%	14%	8%	:	Zone Reached
						:	Zone(1) Close, Zone(3) Open
		36%	64%	66%	64%	:	Zone Resistance
33%	57%	49%				:	Zone Support
22%	51%	100%	65%	23%	8%	:	Zone Reached
						:	Zone(1) Close, Zone(4) Open
			37%	72%	35%	:	Zone Resistance
60%	58%	69%	18%			:	Zone Support
11%	25%	82%	100%	63%	18%	:	Zone Reached
						:	Zone(1) Close, Zone(5) Open
				57%	39%	:	Zone Resistance
67%	25%	75%	52%	21%		:	Zone Support
7%	10%	38%	79%	100%	43%	:	Zone Reached
						:	Zone(1) Close, Zone(6) Open
					25%	:	Zone Resistance
		100%	0%	75%	25%	:	Zone Support
0%	0%	19%	19%	75%	100%	:	Zone Reached
						:	Zone(2) Close, Zone(1) Open
45%	41%	41%	40%	33%	50%	:	Zone Resistance
47%						:	Zone Support
100%	55%	32%	19%	11%	8%	:	Zone Reached
						:	Zone(2) Close, Zone(2) Open
	21%	66%	43%	14%	17%	:	Zone Resistance
47%	21%					:	Zone Support
79%	100%	79%	29%	15%	12%	:	Zone Reached
						:	Zone(2) Close, Zone(3) Open
		31%	62%	79%	29%	:	Zone Resistance
48%	64%	42%				:	Zone Support
21%	58%	100%	70%	26%	5%	:	Zone Reached
						:	Zone(2) Close, Zone(4) Open
			23%	56%	45%	:	Zone Resistance
0%	80%	76%	37%			:	Zone Support
3%	15%	63%	100%	77%	34%	:	Zone Reached
						:	Zone(2) Close, Zone(5) Open
				50%	36%	:	Zone Resistance
0%	67%	73%	52%	18%		:	Zone Support
4%	11%	39%	82%	100%	50%	:	Zone Reached
						:	Zone(2) Close, Zone(6) Open
					39%	:	Zone Resistance
		100%	75%	71%	39%	:	Zone Support
0%	0%	4%	17%	61%	100%	:	Zone Reached
						:	Zone(3) Close, Zone(1) Open
46%	46%	45%	18%	44%	60%	:	Zone Resistance
51%						:	Zone Support
100%	54%	29%	16%	13%	7%	:	Zone Reached
						:	Zone(3) Close, Zone(2) Open
	24%	59%	76%	0%	67%	:	Zone Resistance
47%	36%					:	Zone Support
64%	100%	76%	31%	8%	8%	:	Zone Reached
						:	Zone(3) Close, Zone(3) Open
		29%	58%	60%	40%	:	Zone Resistance
43%	59%	46%				:	Zone Support
22%	54%	100%	71%	30%	12%	:	Zone Reached
						:	Zone(3) Close, Zone(4) Open
			34%	68%	31%	:	Zone Resistance
56%	50%	64%	33%			:	Zone Support
12%	24%	67%	100%	66%	21%	:	Zone Reached
						:	Zone(3) Close, Zone(5) Open
				37%	38%	:	Zone Resistance
29%	12%	58%	60%	30%		:	Zone Support
10%	12%	28%	70%	100%	63%	:	Zone Reached
						:	Zone(3) Close, Zone(6) Open
					40%	:	Zone Resistance
0%	0%	67%	57%	58%	38%	:	Zone Support
4%	4%	11%	26%	62%	100%	:	Zone Reached

Z O N E S (1) - (6)   : ZONE(?) CLOSE, ZONE(?) OPEN

(1)	(2)	(3)	(4)	(5)	(6)	:	
						:	Zone(4) Close, Zone(1) Open
43%	57%	60%	50%	33%	50%	:	Zone Resistance
46%						:	Zone Support
100%	57%	25%	10%	5%	3%	:	Zone Reached
						:	Zone(4) Close, Zone(2) Open
	29%	60%	64%	50%	75%	:	Zone Resistance
43%	31%					:	Zone Support
69%	100%	71%	29%	10%	5%	:	Zone Reached
						:	Zone(4) Close, Zone(3) Open
		28%	61%	54%	33%	:	Zone Resistance
43%	57%	35%				:	Zone Support
28%	65%	100%	73%	27%	12%	:	Zone Reached
						:	Zone(4) Close, Zone(4) Open
			48%	49%	46%	:	Zone Resistance
50%	67%	59%	28%			:	Zone Support
10%	30%	72%	100%	52%	27%	:	Zone Reached
						:	Zone(4) Close, Zone(5) Open
				33%	34%	:	Zone Resistance
40%	55%	42%	61%	35%		:	Zone Support
7%	15%	25%	65%	100%	67%	:	Zone Reached
						:	Zone(4) Close, Zone(6) Open
					35%	:	Zone Resistance
	100%	80%	67%	62%	43%	:	Zone Support
0%	1%	7%	22%	57%	100%	:	Zone Reached
						:	Zone(5) Close, Zone(1) Open
62%	25%	17%	80%	0%	0%	:	Zone Resistance
38%						:	Zone Support
100%	38%	29%	24%	5%	5%	:	Zone Reached
						:	Zone(5) Close, Zone(2) Open
	21%	62%	80%	50%	0%	:	Zone Resistance
65%	39%					:	Zone Support
61%	100%	79%	30%	6%	3%	:	Zone Reached
						:	Zone(5) Close, Zone(3) Open
		31%	66%	73%	25%	:	Zone Resistance
53%	65%	33%				:	Zone Support
23%	67%	100%	69%	23%	6%	:	Zone Reached
						:	Zone(5) Close, Zone(4) Open
			48%	57%	52%	:	Zone Resistance
50%	78%	62%	29%			:	Zone Support
6%	26%	71%	100%	52%	23%	:	Zone Reached
						:	Zone(5) Close, Zone(5) Open
				41%	35%	:	Zone Resistance
33%	62%	27%	54%	17%		:	Zone Support
10%	28%	38%	83%	100%	59%	:	Zone Reached
						:	Zone(5) Close, Zone(6) Open
					45%	:	Zone Resistance
50%	60%	17%	57%	30%	31%	:	Zone Support
7%	17%	21%	48%	69%	100%	:	Zone Reached
						:	Zone(6) Close, Zone(1) Open
57%	60%	50%	50%	100%		:	Zone Resistance
35%						:	Zone Support
100%	43%	17%	9%	4%	0%	:	Zone Reached
						:	Zone(6) Close, Zone(2) Open
	16%	38%	75%	0%	40%	:	Zone Resistance
93%	63%					:	Zone Support
37%	100%	84%	53%	13%	13%	:	Zone Reached
						:	Zone(6) Close, Zone(3) Open
		16%	73%	53%	25%	:	Zone Resistance
25%	72%	43%				:	Zone Support
16%	57%	100%	84%	22%	11%	:	Zone Reached
						:	Zone(6) Close, Zone(4) Open
			56%	75%	33%	:	Zone Resistance
50%	84%	59%	38%			:	Zone Support
4%	26%	62%	100%	44%	11%	:	Zone Reached
						:	Zone(6) Close, Zone(5) Open
				38%	67%	:	Zone Resistance
100%	80%	69%	68%	14%		:	Zone Support
2%	9%	28%	86%	100%	62%	:	Zone Reached
						:	Zone(6) Close, Zone(6) Open
					48%	:	Zone Resistance
67%	40%	38%	56%	44%	33%	:	Zone Support
6%	10%	17%	38%	67%	100%	:	Zone Reached

Z O N E S (1) - (6)   : ZONE(?) CLOSE, ZONE(?) OPEN

(1)	(2)	(3)	(4)	(5)	(6)		
51%	55%	60%	50%	67%	0%	:	Zone(1) Close, Zone(1) Open — Zone Resistance
47%						:	Zone Support
100%	49%	22%	9%	4%	1%	:	Zone Reached
	25%	64%	69%	50%	100%	:	Zone(1) Close, Zone(2) Open — Zone Resistance
45%	32%					:	Zone Support
68%	100%	75%	29%	7%	4%	:	Zone Reached
		30%	65%	70%	54%	:	Zone(1) Close, Zone(3) Open — Zone Resistance
46%	58%	49%				:	Zone Support
21%	51%	100%	70%	25%	7%	:	Zone Reached
			32%	71%	29%	:	Zone(1) Close, Zone(4) Open — Zone Resistance
75%	67%	81%	40%			:	Zone Support
4%	11%	60%	100%	68%	20%	:	Zone Reached
				42%	47%	:	Zone(1) Close, Zone(5) Open — Zone Resistance
50%	67%	67%	54%	29%		:	Zone Support
4%	11%	33%	71%	100%	58%	:	Zone Reached
					26%	:	Zone(1) Close, Zone(6) Open — Zone Resistance
	100%	50%	33%	80%	61%	:	Zone Support
0%	3%	5%	8%	39%	100%	:	Zone Reached
43%	54%	62%	43%	67%	0%	:	Zone(2) Close, Zone(1) Open — Zone Resistance
51%						:	Zone Support
100%	57%	26%	11%	5%	2%	:	Zone Reached
	17%	72%	58%	50%	50%	:	Zone(2) Close, Zone(2) Open — Zone Resistance
38%	33%					:	Zone Support
67%	100%	83%	25%	8%	4%	:	Zone Reached
		35%	64%	58%	55%	:	Zone(2) Close, Zone(3) Open — Zone Resistance
57%	55%	45%				:	Zone Support
25%	55%	100%	66%	23%	10%	:	Zone Reached
			30%	57%	65%	:	Zone(2) Close, Zone(4) Open — Zone Resistance
100%	86%	85%	30%			:	Zone Support
2%	11%	70%	100%	70%	30%	:	Zone Reached
				45%	71%	:	Zone(2) Close, Zone(5) Open — Zone Resistance
0%	50%	64%	56%	19%		:	Zone Support
6%	13%	35%	81%	100%	55%	:	Zone Reached
					43%	:	Zone(2) Close, Zone(6) Open — Zone Resistance
		100%	71%	53%	46%	:	Zone Support
0%	0%	7%	25%	54%	100%	:	Zone Reached
49%	51%	50%	20%	25%	33%	:	Zone(3) Close, Zone(1) Open — Zone Resistance
46%						:	Zone Support
100%	51%	25%	12%	10%	7%	:	Zone Reached
	26%	69%	63%	100%		:	Zone(3) Close, Zone(2) Open — Zone Resistance
41%	35%					:	Zone Support
65%	100%	74%	24%	8%	0%	:	Zone Reached
		31%	60%	63%	44%	:	Zone(3) Close, Zone(3) Open — Zone Resistance
30%	58%	40%				:	Zone Support
25%	60%	100%	69%	28%	10%	:	Zone Reached
			38%	59%	50%	:	Zone(3) Close, Zone(4) Open — Zone Resistance
50%	59%	71%	30%			:	Zone Support
9%	21%	70%	100%	62%	26%	:	Zone Reached
				33%	40%	:	Zone(3) Close, Zone(5) Open — Zone Resistance
100%	50%	78%	58%	28%		:	Zone Support
3%	7%	30%	72%	100%	67%	:	Zone Reached
					49%	:	Zone(3) Close, Zone(6) Open — Zone Resistance
60%	38%	38%	32%	37%	59%	:	Zone Support
7%	11%	18%	26%	41%	100%	:	Zone Reached

```
                              *** YEN ***


              Z O N E S   (1) - (6)        : ZONE(?) CLOSE, ZONE(?) OPEN


        (1)    (2)    (3)    (4)    (5)    (6)
       ----------------------------------------- : Zone(4) Close, Zone(1) Open
        48%    61%    71%    60%     0%     0%    :    Zone Resistance
        45%                                      :    Zone Support
       100%    52%    20%     7%     1%     1%    :    Zone Reached
       ----------------------------------------- : Zone(4) Close, Zone(2) Open
               23%    58%    65%    50%    25%    :    Zone Resistance
        48%    41%                               :    Zone Support
        59%   100%    77%    32%    11%     6%    :    Zone Reached
       ----------------------------------------- : Zone(4) Close, Zone(3) Open
               27%    70%    69%    38%           :    Zone Resistance
        48%    65%    43%                         :    Zone Support
        20%    57%   100%    76%    20%     6%    :    Zone Reached
       ----------------------------------------- : Zone(4) Close, Zone(4) Open
                             44%    53%    53%    :    Zone Resistance
        58%    68%    54%    28%                  :    Zone Support
        10%    33%    72%   100%    56%    26%    :    Zone Reached
       ----------------------------------------- : Zone(4) Close, Zone(5) Open
                             24%    46%           :    Zone Resistance
       100%    40%    55%    70%    27%           :    Zone Support
         6%    10%    22%    73%   100%    76%    :    Zone Reached
       ----------------------------------------- : Zone(4) Close, Zone(6) Open
                                           39%    :    Zone Resistance
              100%    78%    53%    56%    49%    :    Zone Support
         0%     2%    11%    23%    51%   100%    :    Zone Reached
       ----------------------------------------- : Zone(5) Close, Zone(1) Open
        32%    47%    44%    60%    50%   100%    :    Zone Resistance
        56%                                      :    Zone Support
       100%    68%    36%    20%     8%     4%    :    Zone Reached
       ----------------------------------------- : Zone(5) Close, Zone(2) Open
               31%    67%    56%    33%    50%    :    Zone Resistance
        45%    43%                               :    Zone Support
        57%   100%    69%    26%     9%     6%    :    Zone Reached
       ----------------------------------------- : Zone(5) Close, Zone(3) Open
               30%    79%    58%    80%           :    Zone Resistance
        43%    77%    30%                         :    Zone Support
        16%    70%   100%    72%    14%     6%    :    Zone Reached
       ----------------------------------------- : Zone(5) Close, Zone(4) Open
                             42%    61%    50%    :    Zone Resistance
        33%    86%    59%    32%                  :    Zone Support
         4%    28%    68%   100%    57%    22%    :    Zone Reached
       ----------------------------------------- : Zone(5) Close, Zone(5) Open
                             27%    53%           :    Zone Resistance
        67%    50%    62%    47%    27%           :    Zone Support
         7%    15%    39%    73%   100%    73%    :    Zone Reached
       ----------------------------------------- : Zone(5) Close, Zone(6) Open
                                           36%    :    Zone Resistance
        67%    40%    29%    30%    50%    55%    :    Zone Support
         7%    11%    16%    23%    45%   100%    :    Zone Reached
       ----------------------------------------- : Zone(6) Close, Zone(1) Open
        58%    41%    38%    75%     0%     0%    :    Zone Resistance
        48%                                      :    Zone Support
       100%    42%    25%    15%     4%     4%    :    Zone Reached
       ----------------------------------------- : Zone(6) Close, Zone(2) Open
               26%    55%    68%    67%   100%    :    Zone Resistance
        44%    53%                               :    Zone Support
        47%   100%    74%    33%    11%     4%    :    Zone Reached
       ----------------------------------------- : Zone(6) Close, Zone(3) Open
               31%    79%    50%    50%           :    Zone Resistance
        42%    81%    33%                         :    Zone Support
        13%    67%   100%    72%    13%     6%    :    Zone Reached
       ----------------------------------------- : Zone(6) Close, Zone(4) Open
                             50%    57%    63%    :    Zone Resistance
        64%    67%    59%    42%                  :    Zone Support
         8%    24%    58%   100%    50%    22%    :    Zone Reached
       ----------------------------------------- : Zone(6) Close, Zone(5) Open
                             34%    50%           :    Zone Resistance
        67%    73%    35%    67%    15%           :    Zone Support
         5%    18%    28%    85%   100%    66%    :    Zone Reached
       ----------------------------------------- : Zone(6) Close, Zone(6) Open
                                           55%    :    Zone Resistance
       100%    33%    40%    71%    51%    53%    :    Zone Support
         3%     4%     7%    23%    47%   100%    :    Zone Reached
```

*** POUND ***

Z O N E S (1) - (6)   : ZONE(?) CLOSE, ZONE(?) OPEN

(1)	(2)	(3)	(4)	(5)	(6)	:	
						:	Zone(1) Close, Zone(1) Open
50%	62%	70%	0%	33%	50%	:	Zone Resistance
48%						:	Zone Support
100%	50%	19%	8%	6%	4%	:	Zone Reached
						:	Zone(1) Close, Zone(2) Open
	25%	57%	40%	80%	0%	:	Zone Resistance
50%	32%					:	Zone Support
68%	100%	75%	36%	18%	4%	:	Zone Reached
						:	Zone(1) Close, Zone(3) Open
		37%	63%	69%	42%	:	Zone Resistance
36%	69%	53%				:	Zone Support
15%	47%	100%	64%	23%	7%	:	Zone Reached
						:	Zone(1) Close, Zone(4) Open
			41%	70%	50%	:	Zone Resistance
25%	78%	64%	38%			:	Zone Support
5%	22%	62%	100%	59%	18%	:	Zone Reached
						:	Zone(1) Close, Zone(5) Open
				45%	43%	:	Zone Resistance
50%	0%	82%	67%	13%		:	Zone Support
5%	5%	29%	87%	100%	55%	:	Zone Reached
						:	Zone(1) Close, Zone(6) Open
					21%	:	Zone Resistance
0%	0%	0%	0%	80%	64%	:	Zone Support
7%	7%	7%	7%	36%	100%	:	Zone Reached
						:	Zone(2) Close, Zone(1) Open
45%	44%	40%	50%	33%	50%	:	Zone Resistance
39%						:	Zone Support
100%	55%	30%	18%	9%	6%	:	Zone Reached
						:	Zone(2) Close, Zone(2) Open
	17%	60%	69%	33%	50%	:	Zone Resistance
52%	31%					:	Zone Support
69%	100%	83%	36%	8%	6%	:	Zone Reached
						:	Zone(2) Close, Zone(3) Open
		29%	56%	64%	64%	:	Zone Resistance
36%	59%	46%				:	Zone Support
22%	54%	100%	72%	31%	11%	:	Zone Reached
						:	Zone(2) Close, Zone(4) Open
			31%	71%	36%	:	Zone Resistance
60%	72%	61%	35%			:	Zone Support
7%	25%	65%	100%	69%	20%	:	Zone Reached
						:	Zone(2) Close, Zone(5) Open
				44%	42%	:	Zone Resistance
0%	33%	57%	73%	24%		:	Zone Support
6%	9%	21%	76%	100%	56%	:	Zone Reached
						:	Zone(2) Close, Zone(6) Open
					47%	:	Zone Resistance
		100%	50%	75%	53%	:	Zone Support
0%	0%	6%	12%	47%	100%	:	Zone Reached
						:	Zone(3) Close, Zone(1) Open
48%	52%	31%	45%	50%	67%	:	Zone Resistance
50%						:	Zone Support
100%	52%	25%	17%	9%	5%	:	Zone Reached
						:	Zone(3) Close, Zone(2) Open
	14%	58%	55%	57%	50%	:	Zone Resistance
49%	42%					:	Zone Support
58%	100%	86%	36%	16%	7%	:	Zone Reached
						:	Zone(3) Close, Zone(3) Open
		27%	60%	67%	62%	:	Zone Resistance
42%	57%	43%				:	Zone Support
25%	57%	100%	74%	28%	9%	:	Zone Reached
						:	Zone(3) Close, Zone(4) Open
			33%	58%	42%	:	Zone Resistance
37%	54%	59%	41%			:	Zone Support
11%	24%	59%	100%	67%	29%	:	Zone Reached
						:	Zone(3) Close, Zone(5) Open
				34%	34%	:	Zone Resistance
33%	0%	81%	73%	22%		:	Zone Support
4%	4%	21%	78%	100%	66%	:	Zone Reached
						:	Zone(3) Close, Zone(6) Open
					37%	:	Zone Resistance
	100%	80%	55%	54%	51%	:	Zone Support
0%	2%	10%	22%	49%	100%	:	Zone Reached

Z O N E S (1) - (6)   : ZONE(?) CLOSE, ZONE(?) OPEN

(1)	(2)	(3)	(4)	(5)	(6)		
						:	Zone(4) Close, Zone(1) Open
52%	53%	57%	83%	0%	0%	:	Zone Resistance
53%						:	Zone Support
100%	48%	23%	10%	2%	2%	:	Zone Reached
						:	Zone(4) Close, Zone(2) Open
	20%	60%	56%	27%	38%	:	Zone Resistance
66%	35%					:	Zone Support
65%	100%	80%	33%	14%	10%	:	Zone Reached
						:	Zone(4) Close, Zone(3) Open
		29%	59%	71%	21%	:	Zone Resistance
62%	59%	37%				:	Zone Support
26%	63%	100%	72%	28%	8%	:	Zone Reached
						:	Zone(4) Close, Zone(4) Open
			39%	51%	42%	:	Zone Resistance
39%	50%	60%	31%			:	Zone Support
14%	27%	69%	100%	61%	30%	:	Zone Reached
						:	Zone(4) Close, Zone(5) Open
				37%	43%	:	Zone Resistance
50%	82%	56%	60%	16%		:	Zone Support
3%	15%	33%	84%	100%	63%	:	Zone Reached
						:	Zone(4) Close, Zone(6) Open
					38%	:	Zone Resistance
0%	50%	33%	77%	62%	55%	:	Zone Support
1%	3%	4%	17%	45%	100%	:	Zone Reached
						:	Zone(5) Close, Zone(1) Open
25%	67%	83%	100%			:	Zone Resistance
46%						:	Zone Support
100%	75%	25%	4%	0%	0%	:	Zone Reached
						:	Zone(5) Close, Zone(2) Open
	5%	67%	88%			:	Zone Resistance
75%	45%					:	Zone Support
55%	100%	95%	36%	0%	0%	:	Zone Reached
						:	Zone(5) Close, Zone(3) Open
		22%	64%	60%	62%	:	Zone Resistance
74%	60%	36%				:	Zone Support
26%	64%	100%	80%	27%	11%	:	Zone Reached
						:	Zone(5) Close, Zone(4) Open
			43%	57%	45%	:	Zone Resistance
45%	67%	59%	31%			:	Zone Support
9%	28%	69%	100%	57%	25%	:	Zone Reached
						:	Zone(5) Close, Zone(5) Open
				33%	41%	:	Zone Resistance
100%	75%	67%	54%	21%		:	Zone Support
3%	12%	36%	79%	100%	67%	:	Zone Reached
						:	Zone(5) Close, Zone(6) Open
					56%	:	Zone Resistance
0%	0%	86%	53%	32%	39%	:	Zone Support
3%	3%	19%	42%	61%	100%	:	Zone Reached
						:	Zone(6) Close, Zone(1) Open
33%	60%	75%	0%	0%	100%	:	Zone Resistance
47%						:	Zone Support
100%	67%	27%	7%	7%	7%	:	Zone Reached
						:	Zone(6) Close, Zone(2) Open
	29%	66%	70%	0%	67%	:	Zone Resistance
57%	44%					:	Zone Support
56%	100%	71%	24%	7%	7%	:	Zone Reached
						:	Zone(6) Close, Zone(3) Open
		25%	82%	57%	33%	:	Zone Resistance
57%	79%	36%				:	Zone Support
13%	64%	100%	75%	13%	6%	:	Zone Reached
						:	Zone(6) Close, Zone(4) Open
			51%	65%	56%	:	Zone Resistance
62%	82%	65%	37%			:	Zone Support
4%	22%	63%	100%	49%	17%	:	Zone Reached
						:	Zone(6) Close, Zone(5) Open
				28%	46%	:	Zone Resistance
67%	50%	57%	68%	19%		:	Zone Support
6%	11%	26%	81%	100%	72%	:	Zone Reached
						:	Zone(6) Close, Zone(6) Open
					43%	:	Zone Resistance
33%	57%	30%	38%	47%	29%	:	Zone Support
7%	17%	24%	38%	71%	100%	:	Zone Reached

```
                        *** SOYBEANS ***


            Z O N E S  (1) - (6)         : ZONE(?) CLOSE, ZONE(?) OPEN


         (1)    (2)    (3)    (4)    (5)    (6)
      -----------------------------------------  : Zone(1) Close, Zone(1) Open
        30%    44%    33%    33%    25%    67%    :     Zone Resistance
        39%                                       :     Zone Support
       100%    70%    39%    26%    17%    13%    :     Zone Reached
      -----------------------------------------  : Zone(1) Close, Zone(2) Open
               31%    67%    50%    33%    50%    :     Zone Resistance
        26%    27%                                :     Zone Support
        73%   100%    69%    23%    12%     8%    :     Zone Reached
      -----------------------------------------  : Zone(1) Close, Zone(3) Open
                      45%    64%    65%    42%    :     Zone Resistance
        35%    65%    53%                         :     Zone Support
        16%    47%   100%    57%    19%     6%    :     Zone Reached
      -----------------------------------------  : Zone(1) Close, Zone(4) Open
                             37%    82%    50%    :     Zone Resistance
       100%    89%    76%    29%                  :     Zone Support
         2%    17%    71%   100%    63%    12%    :     Zone Reached
      -----------------------------------------  : Zone(1) Close, Zone(5) Open
                             57%    67%           :     Zone Resistance
                     100%    50%    14%           :     Zone Support
         0%     0%    43%    86%   100%    43%    :     Zone Reached
      -----------------------------------------  : Zone(1) Close, Zone(6) Open
                                            0%    :     Zone Resistance
                                          100%    :     Zone Support
         0%     0%     0%     0%     0%   100%    :     Zone Reached
      -----------------------------------------  : Zone(2) Close, Zone(1) Open
        43%    50%     0%     0%     0%    25%    :     Zone Resistance
        50%                                       :     Zone Support
       100%    57%    29%    29%    29%    29%    :     Zone Reached
      -----------------------------------------  : Zone(2) Close, Zone(2) Open
               31%    50%    45%    67%   100%    :     Zone Resistance
        48%    22%                                :     Zone Support
        78%   100%    69%    34%    19%     6%    :     Zone Reached
      -----------------------------------------  : Zone(2) Close, Zone(3) Open
                      34%    53%    67%    29%    :     Zone Resistance
        29%    52%    47%                         :     Zone Support
        25%    53%   100%    67%    31%    10%    :     Zone Reached
      -----------------------------------------  : Zone(2) Close, Zone(4) Open
                             32%    57%    39%    :     Zone Resistance
        17%    25%    79%    39%                  :     Zone Support
        10%    13%    61%   100%    68%    29%    :     Zone Reached
      -----------------------------------------  : Zone(2) Close, Zone(5) Open
                             46%    14%           :     Zone Resistance
                     100%    56%    31%           :     Zone Support
         0%     0%    31%    69%   100%    54%    :     Zone Reached
      -----------------------------------------  : Zone(2) Close, Zone(6) Open
                                          100%    :     Zone Resistance
         0%     0%     0%     0%     0%     0%    :     Zone Support
       100%   100%   100%   100%   100%   100%    :     Zone Reached
      -----------------------------------------  : Zone(3) Close, Zone(1) Open
        45%    25%    33%    17%    20%    25%    :     Zone Resistance
        36%                                       :     Zone Support
       100%    55%    41%    27%    23%    18%    :     Zone Reached
      -----------------------------------------  : Zone(3) Close, Zone(2) Open
               31%    39%    32%    53%    14%    :     Zone Resistance
        26%    35%                                :     Zone Support
        65%   100%    69%    42%    29%    13%    :     Zone Reached
      -----------------------------------------  : Zone(3) Close, Zone(3) Open
                      28%    46%    73%    42%    :     Zone Resistance
        36%    59%    41%                         :     Zone Support
        24%    59%   100%    73%    38%    10%    :     Zone Reached
      -----------------------------------------  : Zone(3) Close, Zone(4) Open
                             32%    56%    44%    :     Zone Resistance
        17%    60%    60%    37%                  :     Zone Support
        10%    25%    63%   100%    68%    30%    :     Zone Reached
      -----------------------------------------  : Zone(3) Close, Zone(5) Open
                             25%    39%           :     Zone Resistance
        67%    57%    46%    61%    25%           :     Zone Support
         7%    16%    30%    75%   100%    75%    :     Zone Reached
      -----------------------------------------  : Zone(3) Close, Zone(6) Open
                                           40%    :     Zone Resistance
       100%     0%    67%    25%    20%    67%    :     Zone Support
         7%     7%    20%    27%    33%   100%    :     Zone Reached
```

Z O N E S (1) - (6)   : ZONE(?) CLOSE, ZONE(?) OPEN

(1)	(2)	(3)	(4)	(5)	(6)		
						:	Zone(4) Close, Zone(1) Open
50%	50%	25%	33%	50%	0%	:	Zone Resistance
44%						:	Zone Support
100%	50%	25%	19%	12%	6%	:	Zone Reached
						:	Zone(4) Close, Zone(2) Open
	39%	32%	37%	50%	33%	:	Zone Resistance
28%	30%					:	Zone Support
70%	100%	61%	41%	26%	13%	:	Zone Reached
						:	Zone(4) Close, Zone(3) Open
		26%	53%	52%	58%	:	Zone Resistance
37%	61%	30%				:	Zone Support
27%	70%	100%	74%	34%	17%	:	Zone Reached
						:	Zone(4) Close, Zone(4) Open
			45%	53%	45%	:	Zone Resistance
29%	50%	56%	28%			:	Zone Support
16%	31%	71%	99%	56%	26%	:	Zone Reached
						:	Zone(4) Close, Zone(5) Open
				21%	39%	:	Zone Resistance
25%	33%	54%	68%	35%		:	Zone Support
6%	10%	21%	65%	100%	79%	:	Zone Reached
						:	Zone(4) Close, Zone(6) Open
					33%	:	Zone Resistance
50%	0%	50%	20%	62%	57%	:	Zone Support
7%	7%	13%	17%	43%	100%	:	Zone Reached
						:	Zone(5) Close, Zone(1) Open
0%	33%	50%	100%			:	Zone Resistance
67%						:	Zone Support
100%	100%	67%	33%	0%	0%	:	Zone Reached
						:	Zone(5) Close, Zone(2) Open
	27%	45%	71%	100%		:	Zone Resistance
25%	47%					:	Zone Support
53%	100%	73%	47%	7%	0%	:	Zone Reached
						:	Zone(5) Close, Zone(3) Open
		28%	58%	55%	40%	:	Zone Resistance
30%	62%	26%				:	Zone Support
28%	74%	100%	72%	31%	14%	:	Zone Reached
						:	Zone(5) Close, Zone(4) Open
			59%	60%	31%	:	Zone Resistance
22%	65%	56%	30%			:	Zone Support
11%	31%	70%	100%	41%	17%	:	Zone Reached
						:	Zone(5) Close, Zone(5) Open
				34%	57%	:	Zone Resistance
0%	83%	45%	59%	16%		:	Zone Support
3%	19%	34%	84%	100%	66%	:	Zone Reached
						:	Zone(5) Close, Zone(6) Open
					38%	:	Zone Resistance
0%	50%	0%	50%	33%	62%	:	Zone Support
6%	12%	12%	25%	38%	100%	:	Zone Reached
						:	Zone(6) Close, Zone(1) Open
43%	50%	0%	0%	0%	50%	:	Zone Resistance
29%						:	Zone Support
100%	57%	29%	29%	29%	29%	:	Zone Reached
						:	Zone(6) Close, Zone(2) Open
	38%	40%	50%	33%	0%	:	Zone Resistance
25%	50%					:	Zone Support
50%	100%	62%	38%	19%	12%	:	Zone Reached
						:	Zone(6) Close, Zone(3) Open
		34%	79%	67%	33%	:	Zone Resistance
56%	62%	34%				:	Zone Support
25%	66%	100%	66%	14%	5%	:	Zone Reached
						:	Zone(6) Close, Zone(4) Open
			65%	59%	42%	:	Zone Resistance
43%	82%	72%	37%			:	Zone Support
3%	18%	63%	100%	35%	14%	:	Zone Reached
						:	Zone(6) Close, Zone(5) Open
				45%	25%	:	Zone Resistance
0%	80%	55%	54%	17%		:	Zone Support
3%	17%	38%	83%	100%	55%	:	Zone Reached
						:	Zone(6) Close, Zone(6) Open
					50%	:	Zone Resistance
25%	20%	29%	36%	0%	58%	:	Zone Support
15%	19%	27%	42%	42%	100%	:	Zone Reached

Z O N E S (1) - (6)   : ZONE(?) CLOSE, ZONE(?) OPEN

(1)	(2)	(3)	(4)	(5)	(6)		
						:	Zone(1) Close, Zone(1) Open
43%	46%	71%	0%	0%	50%	:	Zone Resistance
30%						:	Zone Support
100%	57%	30%	13%	9%	9%	:	Zone Reached
						:	Zone(1) Close, Zone(2) Open
	34%	72%	38%	50%	0%	:	Zone Resistance
39%	26%					:	Zone Support
74%	100%	66%	21%	11%	5%	:	Zone Reached
						:	Zone(1) Close, Zone(3) Open
		51%	63%	70%	36%	:	Zone Resistance
43%	58%	48%				:	Zone Support
22%	52%	100%	51%	17%	5%	:	Zone Reached
						:	Zone(1) Close, Zone(4) Open
			47%	75%	50%	:	Zone Resistance
0%	71%	79%	27%			:	Zone Support
4%	16%	73%	100%	53%	13%	:	Zone Reached
						:	Zone(1) Close, Zone(5) Open
				64%	75%	:	Zone Resistance
50%	33%	62%	20%	9%		:	Zone Support
18%	27%	73%	91%	100%	36%	:	Zone Reached
						:	Zone(1) Close, Zone(6) Open
					0%	:	Zone Resistance
100%	0%	0%	0%	0%	67%	:	Zone Support
33%	33%	33%	33%	33%	100%	:	Zone Reached
						:	Zone(2) Close, Zone(1) Open
50%	20%	38%	0%	40%	33%	:	Zone Resistance
50%						:	Zone Support
100%	50%	40%	25%	25%	15%	:	Zone Reached
						:	Zone(2) Close, Zone(2) Open
	35%	70%	56%	25%	0%	:	Zone Resistance
35%	20%					:	Zone Support
80%	100%	65%	20%	9%	7%	:	Zone Reached
						:	Zone(2) Close, Zone(3) Open
		38%	50%	74%	47%	:	Zone Resistance
38%	65%	36%				:	Zone Support
22%	64%	100%	63%	31%	8%	:	Zone Reached
						:	Zone(2) Close, Zone(4) Open
			35%	47%	56%	:	Zone Resistance
33%	57%	62%	30%			:	Zone Support
11%	27%	70%	100%	65%	34%	:	Zone Reached
						:	Zone(2) Close, Zone(5) Open
				45%	33%	:	Zone Resistance
50%	50%	50%	60%	9%		:	Zone Support
9%	18%	36%	91%	100%	55%	:	Zone Reached
						:	Zone(2) Close, Zone(6) Open
					50%	:	Zone Resistance
			100%	67%	25%	:	Zone Support
0%	0%	0%	25%	75%	100%	:	Zone Reached
						:	Zone(3) Close, Zone(1) Open
44%	67%	33%	50%	0%	0%	:	Zone Resistance
25%						:	Zone Support
100%	56%	19%	12%	6%	6%	:	Zone Reached
						:	Zone(3) Close, Zone(2) Open
	21%	42%	38%	33%	58%	:	Zone Resistance
44%	33%					:	Zone Support
67%	98%	78%	45%	28%	19%	:	Zone Reached
						:	Zone(3) Close, Zone(3) Open
		37%	53%	56%	47%	:	Zone Resistance
37%	49%	35%				:	Zone Support
33%	65%	100%	64%	29%	13%	:	Zone Reached
						:	Zone(3) Close, Zone(4) Open
			36%	51%	46%	:	Zone Resistance
52%	61%	62%	32%			:	Zone Support
10%	26%	68%	100%	64%	31%	:	Zone Reached
						:	Zone(3) Close, Zone(5) Open
				23%	35%	:	Zone Resistance
50%	60%	55%	61%	36%		:	Zone Support
5%	11%	25%	64%	100%	77%	:	Zone Reached
						:	Zone(3) Close, Zone(6) Open
					57%	:	Zone Resistance
	100%	67%	40%	29%	39%	:	Zone Support
0%	9%	26%	43%	61%	100%	:	Zone Reached

ZONES (1) - (6)   : ZONE(?) CLOSE, ZONE(?) OPEN

(1)	(2)	(3)	(4)	(5)	(6)		
						:	Zone(4) Close, Zone(1) Open
43%	50%	75%	0%	0%	0%	:	Zone Resistance
43%						:	Zone Support
100%	57%	29%	7%	7%	7%	:	Zone Reached
						:	Zone(4) Close, Zone(2) Open
	29%	53%	50%	43%	75%	:	Zone Resistance
55%	31%					:	Zone Support
69%	100%	71%	33%	17%	10%	:	Zone Reached
						:	Zone(4) Close, Zone(3) Open
		35%	48%	39%	37%	:	Zone Resistance
46%	51%	30%				:	Zone Support
34%	70%	100%	65%	33%	20%	:	Zone Reached
						:	Zone(4) Close, Zone(4) Open
			47%	50%	43%	:	Zone Resistance
46%	62%	46%	28%			:	Zone Support
15%	39%	72%	100%	53%	27%	:	Zone Reached
						:	Zone(4) Close, Zone(5) Open
				19%	41%	:	Zone Resistance
33%	40%	67%	55%	38%		:	Zone Support
6%	9%	28%	61%	98%	81%	:	Zone Reached
						:	Zone(4) Close, Zone(6) Open
					43%	:	Zone Resistance
40%	17%	14%	30%	33%	46%	:	Zone Support
18%	21%	25%	36%	54%	100%	:	Zone Reached
						:	Zone(5) Close, Zone(1) Open
67%	50%	0%	0%	100%		:	Zone Resistance
33%						:	Zone Support
100%	33%	17%	17%	17%	0%	:	Zone Reached
						:	Zone(5) Close, Zone(2) Open
	27%	45%	50%	33%	100%	:	Zone Resistance
40%	33%					:	Zone Support
67%	100%	73%	40%	20%	13%	:	Zone Reached
						:	Zone(5) Close, Zone(3) Open
		41%	52%	47%	50%	:	Zone Resistance
47%	61%	29%				:	Zone Support
28%	71%	100%	61%	28%	14%	:	Zone Reached
						:	Zone(5) Close, Zone(4) Open
			50%	63%	44%	:	Zone Resistance
64%	77%	59%	37%			:	Zone Support
6%	26%	63%	100%	50%	18%	:	Zone Reached
						:	Zone(5) Close, Zone(5) Open
				23%	42%	:	Zone Resistance
0%	57%	53%	53%	26%		:	Zone Support
7%	16%	35%	74%	100%	77%	:	Zone Reached
						:	Zone(5) Close, Zone(6) Open
					56%	:	Zone Resistance
0%	25%	0%	69%	24%	32%	:	Zone Support
12%	16%	16%	52%	68%	100%	:	Zone Reached
						:	Zone(6) Close, Zone(1) Open
60%	0%	50%	0%	0%	0%	:	Zone Resistance
60%						:	Zone Support
100%	40%	40%	20%	20%	20%	:	Zone Reached
						:	Zone(6) Close, Zone(2) Open
	58%	75%	33%	0%	100%	:	Zone Resistance
31%	32%					:	Zone Support
68%	100%	42%	16%	5%	5%	:	Zone Reached
						:	Zone(6) Close, Zone(3) Open
		37%	78%	50%	40%	:	Zone Resistance
50%	64%	38%				:	Zone Support
23%	62%	100%	63%	14%	7%	:	Zone Reached
						:	Zone(6) Close, Zone(4) Open
			58%	58%	39%	:	Zone Resistance
42%	75%	64%	41%			:	Zone Support
5%	21%	59%	100%	42%	18%	:	Zone Reached
						:	Zone(6) Close, Zone(5) Open
				36%	22%	:	Zone Resistance
0%	0%	71%	61%	36%		:	Zone Support
7%	7%	25%	64%	100%	64%	:	Zone Reached
						:	Zone(6) Close, Zone(6) Open
					46%	:	Zone Resistance
33%	40%	17%	25%	27%	61%	:	Zone Support
11%	18%	21%	29%	39%	100%	:	Zone Reached

Z O N E S (1) - (6)   : ZONE(?) CLOSE, ZONE(?) OPEN

(1)	(2)	(3)	(4)	(5)	(6)		
						:	Zone(1) Close, Zone(1) Open
42%	45%	67%	0%	100%		:	Zone Resistance
32%						:	Zone Support
100%	58%	32%	11%	11%	0%	:	Zone Reached
						:	Zone(1) Close, Zone(2) Open
	26%	76%	14%	17%	40%	:	Zone Resistance
40%	36%					:	Zone Support
64%	100%	74%	18%	15%	13%	:	Zone Reached
						:	Zone(1) Close, Zone(3) Open
		46%	58%	82%	18%	:	Zone Resistance
33%	65%	46%				:	Zone Support
19%	54%	100%	55%	22%	4%	:	Zone Reached
						:	Zone(1) Close, Zone(4) Open
			47%	65%	78%	:	Zone Resistance
57%	53%	64%	14%			:	Zone Support
14%	31%	86%	100%	53%	18%	:	Zone Reached
						:	Zone(1) Close, Zone(5) Open
				25%	50%	:	Zone Resistance
	100%	67%	50%	25%		:	Zone Support
0%	12%	38%	75%	100%	75%	:	Zone Reached
						:	Zone(1) Close, Zone(6) Open
					50%	:	Zone Resistance
100%	0%	50%	50%	20%	17%	:	Zone Support
17%	17%	33%	67%	83%	100%	:	Zone Reached
						:	Zone(2) Close, Zone(1) Open
44%	20%	25%	33%	0%	50%	:	Zone Resistance
56%						:	Zone Support
100%	56%	44%	33%	22%	22%	:	Zone Reached
						:	Zone(2) Close, Zone(2) Open
	35%	68%	43%	75%	0%	:	Zone Resistance
27%	24%					:	Zone Support
76%	100%	65%	21%	12%	3%	:	Zone Reached
						:	Zone(2) Close, Zone(3) Open
		42%	54%	64%	36%	:	Zone Resistance
46%	47%	39%				:	Zone Support
32%	61%	100%	60%	26%	9%	:	Zone Reached
						:	Zone(2) Close, Zone(4) Open
			37%	58%	57%	:	Zone Resistance
0%	74%	58%	19%			:	Zone Support
9%	34%	81%	100%	63%	27%	:	Zone Reached
						:	Zone(2) Close, Zone(5) Open
				31%	27%	:	Zone Resistance
0%	0%	50%	64%	31%		:	Zone Support
12%	12%	25%	69%	100%	69%	:	Zone Reached
						:	Zone(2) Close, Zone(6) Open
					0%	:	Zone Resistance
				100%	33%	:	Zone Support
0%	0%	0%	0%	67%	100%	:	Zone Reached
						:	Zone(3) Close, Zone(1) Open
44%	67%	67%	0%	0%	0%	:	Zone Resistance
19%						:	Zone Support
100%	56%	19%	6%	6%	6%	:	Zone Reached
						:	Zone(3) Close, Zone(2) Open
	33%	46%	52%	40%	33%	:	Zone Resistance
38%	28%					:	Zone Support
72%	100%	67%	36%	17%	10%	:	Zone Reached
						:	Zone(3) Close, Zone(3) Open
		29%	47%	50%	53%	:	Zone Resistance
42%	52%	43%				:	Zone Support
28%	57%	100%	72%	37%	18%	:	Zone Reached
						:	Zone(3) Close, Zone(4) Open
			38%	52%	44%	:	Zone Resistance
22%	54%	57%	27%			:	Zone Support
14%	32%	73%	100%	62%	30%	:	Zone Reached
						:	Zone(3) Close, Zone(5) Open
				46%	58%	:	Zone Resistance
0%	44%	36%	55%	11%		:	Zone Support
14%	26%	40%	89%	100%	54%	:	Zone Reached
						:	Zone(3) Close, Zone(6) Open
					40%	:	Zone Resistance
	100%	67%	40%	38%	60%	:	Zone Support
0%	5%	15%	25%	40%	100%	:	Zone Reached

*** BEAN OIL ***

Z O N E S (1) - (6)   : ZONE(?) CLOSE, ZONE(?) OPEN

(1)	(2)	(3)	(4)	(5)	(6)	
						: Zone(4) Close, Zone(1) Open
62%	40%	33%	50%	100%		: Zone Resistance
31%						: Zone Support
100%	38%	23%	15%	8%	0%	: Zone Reached
						: Zone(4) Close, Zone(2) Open
	31%	76%	38%	50%	50%	: Zone Resistance
40%	29%					: Zone Support
71%	100%	69%	19%	10%	5%	: Zone Reached
						: Zone(4) Close, Zone(3) Open
		25%	56%	52%	44%	: Zone Resistance
57%	58%	38%				: Zone Support
26%	62%	100%	76%	33%	16%	: Zone Reached
						: Zone(4) Close, Zone(4) Open
			42%	40%	43%	: Zone Resistance
30%	68%	47%	30%			: Zone Support
12%	37%	70%	100%	58%	35%	: Zone Reached
						: Zone(4) Close, Zone(5) Open
				29%	41%	: Zone Resistance
25%	60%	52%	40%	27%		: Zone Support
8%	21%	44%	73%	100%	71%	: Zone Reached
						: Zone(4) Close, Zone(6) Open
					48%	: Zone Resistance
	100%	50%	71%	46%	38%	: Zone Support
0%	5%	10%	33%	62%	100%	: Zone Reached
						: Zone(5) Close, Zone(1) Open
0%	75%	0%	100%			: Zone Resistance
25%						: Zone Support
100%	100%	25%	25%	0%	0%	: Zone Reached
						: Zone(5) Close, Zone(2) Open
	33%	30%	86%	100%		: Zone Resistance
17%	60%					: Zone Support
40%	100%	67%	47%	7%	0%	: Zone Reached
						: Zone(5) Close, Zone(3) Open
		32%	65%	72%	60%	: Zone Resistance
38%	57%	36%				: Zone Support
27%	64%	100%	68%	23%	6%	: Zone Reached
						: Zone(5) Close, Zone(4) Open
			47%	52%	46%	: Zone Resistance
53%	70%	57%	37%			: Zone Support
8%	27%	63%	100%	53%	25%	: Zone Reached
						: Zone(5) Close, Zone(5) Open
				39%	50%	: Zone Resistance
33%	45%	15%	46%	27%		: Zone Support
18%	33%	39%	73%	100%	61%	: Zone Reached
						: Zone(5) Close, Zone(6) Open
					56%	: Zone Resistance
50%	50%	20%	17%	25%	50%	: Zone Support
12%	25%	31%	38%	50%	100%	: Zone Reached
						: Zone(6) Close, Zone(1) Open
25%	33%	0%	0%	0%	100%	: Zone Resistance
50%						: Zone Support
100%	75%	50%	75%	50%	50%	: Zone Reached
						: Zone(6) Close, Zone(2) Open
	14%	50%	67%	0%	0%	: Zone Resistance
40%	29%					: Zone Support
71%	100%	86%	43%	14%	14%	: Zone Reached
						: Zone(6) Close, Zone(3) Open
		24%	55%	58%	75%	: Zone Resistance
46%	58%	44%				: Zone Support
24%	56%	100%	76%	35%	15%	: Zone Reached
						: Zone(6) Close, Zone(4) Open
			55%	56%	52%	: Zone Resistance
25%	85%	64%	40%			: Zone Support
3%	22%	60%	100%	45%	20%	: Zone Reached
						: Zone(6) Close, Zone(5) Open
				28%	22%	: Zone Resistance
	100%	50%	82%	12%		: Zone Support
0%	8%	16%	88%	100%	72%	: Zone Reached
						: Zone(6) Close, Zone(6) Open
					48%	: Zone Resistance
20%	29%	0%	12%	43%	39%	: Zone Support
22%	30%	30%	35%	61%	100%	: Zone Reached

*** WHEAT ***

ZONES (1) - (6)   : ZONE(?) CLOSE, ZONE(?) OPEN

(1)	(2)	(3)	(4)	(5)	(6)	:	Description
						:	Zone(1) Close, Zone(1) Open
17%	60%	50%	0%	100%		:	Zone Resistance
50%						:	Zone Support
100%	83%	33%	17%	17%	0%	:	Zone Reached
						:	Zone(1) Close, Zone(2) Open
	22%	67%	57%	50%	100%	:	Zone Resistance
39%	22%					:	Zone Support
78%	100%	78%	30%	9%	4%	:	Zone Reached
						:	Zone(1) Close, Zone(3) Open
		42%	70%	80%	67%	:	Zone Resistance
38%	62%	51%				:	Zone Support
19%	49%	100%	59%	17%	3%	:	Zone Reached
						:	Zone(1) Close, Zone(4) Open
			52%	79%	50%	:	Zone Resistance
60%	44%	73%	18%			:	Zone Support
12%	22%	82%	100%	48%	10%	:	Zone Reached
						:	Zone(1) Close, Zone(5) Open
				50%	50%	:	Zone Resistance
100%	50%	50%	43%	12%		:	Zone Support
12%	25%	50%	88%	100%	50%	:	Zone Reached
						:	Zone(1) Close, Zone(6) Open
						:	Zone Resistance
						:	Zone Support
							Zone Reached
						:	Zone(2) Close, Zone(1) Open
62%	0%	67%	100%			:	Zone Resistance
50%						:	Zone Support
100%	38%	38%	12%	0%	0%	:	Zone Reached
						:	Zone(2) Close, Zone(2) Open
	18%	78%	60%	100%		:	Zone Resistance
39%	21%					:	Zone Support
79%	97%	79%	17%	7%	0%	:	Zone Reached
						:	Zone(2) Close, Zone(3) Open
		33%	52%	72%	38%	:	Zone Resistance
40%	53%	47%				:	Zone Support
25%	53%	100%	69%	31%	9%	:	Zone Reached
						:	Zone(2) Close, Zone(4) Open
			35%	61%	75%	:	Zone Resistance
80%	64%	56%	33%			:	Zone Support
10%	29%	67%	100%	65%	25%	:	Zone Reached
						:	Zone(2) Close, Zone(5) Open
				67%	25%	:	Zone Resistance
33%	50%	25%	27%	8%		:	Zone Support
25%	50%	67%	92%	100%	33%	:	Zone Reached
						:	Zone(2) Close, Zone(6) Open
					40%	:	Zone Resistance
			100%	0%	80%	:	Zone Support
0%	0%	0%	20%	20%	100%	:	Zone Reached
						:	Zone(3) Close, Zone(1) Open
39%	36%	71%	50%	0%	0%	:	Zone Resistance
61%						:	Zone Support
100%	61%	39%	11%	6%	6%	:	Zone Reached
						:	Zone(3) Close, Zone(2) Open
	17%	53%	32%	33%	50%	:	Zone Resistance
62%	28%					:	Zone Support
72%	98%	81%	40%	26%	17%	:	Zone Reached
						:	Zone(3) Close, Zone(3) Open
		32%	48%	67%	42%	:	Zone Resistance
36%	51%	39%				:	Zone Support
30%	61%	100%	70%	35%	11%	:	Zone Reached
						:	Zone(3) Close, Zone(4) Open
			37%	47%	37%	:	Zone Resistance
40%	57%	49%	39%			:	Zone Support
14%	31%	61%	100%	63%	33%	:	Zone Reached
						:	Zone(3) Close, Zone(5) Open
				41%	59%	:	Zone Resistance
40%	38%	38%	50%	10%		:	Zone Support
17%	28%	45%	90%	100%	59%	:	Zone Reached
						:	Zone(3) Close, Zone(6) Open
					36%	:	Zone Resistance
		100%	50%	67%	45%	:	Zone Support
0%	0%	9%	18%	55%	100%	:	Zone Reached

```
Z O N E S  (1) - (6)          : ZONE(?) CLOSE, ZONE(?) OPEN
```

(1)	(2)	(3)	(4)	(5)	(6)		
						:	Zone(4) Close, Zone(1) Open
50%	33%	50%	50%	0%	0%	:	Zone Resistance
42%						:	Zone Support
100%	50%	33%	17%	8%	8%	:	Zone Reached
						:	Zone(4) Close, Zone(2) Open
	16%	35%	67%	40%	67%	:	Zone Resistance
45%	29%					:	Zone Support
71%	100%	84%	58%	16%	10%	:	Zone Reached
						:	Zone(4) Close, Zone(3) Open
		33%	58%	56%	43%	:	Zone Resistance
49%	54%	32%				:	Zone Support
32%	68%	100%	69%	28%	12%	:	Zone Reached
						:	Zone(4) Close, Zone(4) Open
			43%	49%	35%	:	Zone Resistance
62%	60%	54%	28%			:	Zone Support
13%	33%	72%	100%	57%	29%	:	Zone Reached
						:	Zone(4) Close, Zone(5) Open
				31%	54%	:	Zone Resistance
25%	56%	31%	52%	23%		:	Zone Support
11%	26%	37%	77%	100%	69%	:	Zone Reached
						:	Zone(4) Close, Zone(6) Open
					65%	:	Zone Resistance
0%	0%	0%	90%	23%	24%	:	Zone Support
6%	6%	6%	59%	76%	100%	:	Zone Reached
						:	Zone(5) Close, Zone(1) Open
100%						:	Zone Resistance
0%						:	Zone Support
100%	0%	0%	0%	0%	0%	:	Zone Reached
						:	Zone(5) Close, Zone(2) Open
	8%	55%	33%	100%		:	Zone Resistance
60%	58%					:	Zone Support
42%	100%	92%	50%	25%	0%	:	Zone Reached
						:	Zone(5) Close, Zone(3) Open
		19%	76%	43%	12%	:	Zone Resistance
56%	64%	38%				:	Zone Support
22%	62%	100%	81%	19%	11%	:	Zone Reached
						:	Zone(5) Close, Zone(4) Open
			46%	49%	41%	:	Zone Resistance
42%	65%	48%	42%			:	Zone Support
11%	30%	58%	99%	55%	28%	:	Zone Reached
						:	Zone(5) Close, Zone(5) Open
				42%	57%	:	Zone Resistance
	100%	67%	53%	21%		:	Zone Support
0%	12%	38%	79%	100%	58%	:	Zone Reached
						:	Zone(5) Close, Zone(6) Open
					20%	:	Zone Resistance
100%	0%	0%	0%	67%	40%	:	Zone Support
20%	20%	20%	20%	60%	100%	:	Zone Reached
						:	Zone(6) Close, Zone(1) Open
0%	50%	0%	0%	0%	0%	:	Zone Resistance
100%						:	Zone Support
100%	100%	50%	50%	50%	50%	:	Zone Reached
						:	Zone(6) Close, Zone(2) Open
	33%	50%	0%	100%		:	Zone Resistance
25%	33%					:	Zone Support
67%	100%	67%	33%	33%	0%	:	Zone Reached
						:	Zone(6) Close, Zone(3) Open
		20%	80%	71%	100%	:	Zone Resistance
0%	91%	50%				:	Zone Support
5%	50%	100%	80%	16%	5%	:	Zone Reached
						:	Zone(6) Close, Zone(4) Open
			55%	60%	29%	:	Zone Resistance
50%	78%	69%	36%			:	Zone Support
4%	20%	64%	100%	45%	18%	:	Zone Reached
						:	Zone(6) Close, Zone(5) Open
				16%	44%	:	Zone Resistance
100%	83%	25%	50%	16%		:	Zone Support
5%	32%	42%	84%	100%	84%	:	Zone Reached
						:	Zone(6) Close, Zone(6) Open
					56%	:	Zone Resistance
100%	67%	25%	20%	29%	22%	:	Zone Support
11%	33%	44%	56%	78%	100%	:	Zone Reached

ZONES (1) - (6)   : ZONE(?) CLOSE, ZONE(?) OPEN

(1)	(2)	(3)	(4)	(5)	(6)		
						:	Zone(1) Close, Zone(1) Open
61%	29%	60%	0%	100%		:	Zone Resistance
39%						:	Zone Support
100%	39%	28%	11%	11%	0%	:	Zone Reached
						:	Zone(1) Close, Zone(2) Open
	27%	66%	27%	75%	0%	:	Zone Resistance
39%	25%					:	Zone Support
75%	100%	73%	25%	18%	5%	:	Zone Reached
						:	Zone(1) Close, Zone(3) Open
		47%	66%	75%	64%	:	Zone Resistance
39%	64%	44%				:	Zone Support
20%	56%	100%	55%	16%	4%	:	Zone Reached
						:	Zone(1) Close, Zone(4) Open
			36%	69%	67%	:	Zone Resistance
50%	57%	71%	21%			:	Zone Support
10%	23%	79%	100%	64%	20%	:	Zone Reached
						:	Zone(1) Close, Zone(5) Open
				67%	33%	:	Zone Resistance
		100%	57%	22%		:	Zone Support
0%	0%	33%	78%	100%	33%	:	Zone Reached
						:	Zone(1) Close, Zone(6) Open
					60%	:	Zone Resistance
50%	0%	0%	50%	20%	0%	:	Zone Support
40%	40%	40%	80%	100%	100%	:	Zone Reached
						:	Zone(2) Close, Zone(1) Open
62%	0%	67%	0%	0%	100%	:	Zone Resistance
38%						:	Zone Support
100%	38%	38%	12%	12%	12%	:	Zone Reached
						:	Zone(2) Close, Zone(2) Open
	22%	61%	40%	44%	60%	:	Zone Resistance
46%	20%					:	Zone Support
80%	100%	78%	31%	18%	10%	:	Zone Reached
						:	Zone(2) Close, Zone(3) Open
		48%	44%	71%	35%	:	Zone Resistance
31%	53%	35%				:	Zone Support
30%	65%	100%	57%	27%	8%	:	Zone Reached
						:	Zone(2) Close, Zone(4) Open
			23%	59%	44%	:	Zone Resistance
20%	67%	62%	32%			:	Zone Support
9%	26%	68%	100%	77%	32%	:	Zone Reached
						:	Zone(2) Close, Zone(5) Open
				25%	50%	:	Zone Resistance
50%	33%	25%	50%	33%		:	Zone Support
15%	23%	31%	62%	92%	77%	:	Zone Reached
						:	Zone(2) Close, Zone(6) Open
					57%	:	Zone Resistance
33%	0%	0%	25%	0%	43%	:	Zone Support
43%	43%	43%	57%	57%	100%	:	Zone Reached
						:	Zone(3) Close, Zone(1) Open
73%	50%	0%	100%			:	Zone Resistance
13%						:	Zone Support
100%	27%	13%	13%	0%	0%	:	Zone Reached
						:	Zone(3) Close, Zone(2) Open
	29%	56%	25%	56%	75%	:	Zone Resistance
39%	26%					:	Zone Support
74%	100%	71%	32%	24%	11%	:	Zone Reached
						:	Zone(3) Close, Zone(3) Open
		42%	48%	55%	42%	:	Zone Resistance
25%	54%	38%				:	Zone Support
28%	62%	100%	62%	29%	13%	:	Zone Reached
						:	Zone(3) Close, Zone(4) Open
			36%	49%	38%	:	Zone Resistance
50%	66%	55%	36%			:	Zone Support
10%	29%	64%	99%	64%	33%	:	Zone Reached
						:	Zone(3) Close, Zone(5) Open
				30%	42%	:	Zone Resistance
0%	88%	56%	57%	22%		:	Zone Support
2%	15%	33%	78%	100%	70%	:	Zone Reached
						:	Zone(3) Close, Zone(6) Open
					31%	:	Zone Resistance
	100%	50%	33%	70%	38%	:	Zone Support
0%	6%	12%	19%	62%	100%	:	Zone Reached

*** CORN ***

ZONES (1) - (6)   : ZONE(?) CLOSE, ZONE(?) OPEN

(1)	(2)	(3)	(4)	(5)	(6)		
						:	Zone(4) Close, Zone(1) Open
42%	55%	60%	0%	50%	100%	:	Zone Resistance
26%						:	Zone Support
100%	58%	26%	11%	11%	5%	:	Zone Reached
						:	Zone(4) Close, Zone(2) Open
	39%	52%	67%	25%	67%	:	Zone Resistance
23%	24%					:	Zone Support
76%	100%	61%	29%	10%	7%	:	Zone Reached
						:	Zone(4) Close, Zone(3) Open
		36%	54%	53%	52%	:	Zone Resistance
38%	57%	37%				:	Zone Support
27%	63%	100%	67%	28%	13%	:	Zone Reached
						:	Zone(4) Close, Zone(4) Open
			41%	47%	40%	:	Zone Resistance
21%	74%	55%	35%			:	Zone Support
8%	29%	65%	100%	59%	31%	:	Zone Reached
						:	Zone(4) Close, Zone(5) Open
				34%	51%	:	Zone Resistance
40%	29%	59%	57%	25%		:	Zone Support
9%	13%	32%	75%	100%	66%	:	Zone Reached
						:	Zone(4) Close, Zone(6) Open
					37%	:	Zone Resistance
	100%	67%	67%	40%	50%	:	Zone Support
0%	3%	10%	30%	50%	100%	:	Zone Reached
						:	Zone(5) Close, Zone(1) Open
75%	0%	100%				:	Zone Resistance
25%						:	Zone Support
100%	25%	25%	0%	0%	0%	:	Zone Reached
						:	Zone(5) Close, Zone(2) Open
	30%	43%	75%	0%	0%	:	Zone Resistance
50%	20%					:	Zone Support
80%	100%	70%	40%	10%	10%	:	Zone Reached
						:	Zone(5) Close, Zone(3) Open
		39%	57%	42%	36%	:	Zone Resistance
29%	52%	35%				:	Zone Support
31%	65%	100%	64%	25%	14%	:	Zone Reached
						:	Zone(5) Close, Zone(4) Open
			46%	59%	37%	:	Zone Resistance
7%	74%	57%	37%			:	Zone Support
7%	27%	63%	100%	54%	22%	:	Zone Reached
						:	Zone(5) Close, Zone(5) Open
				29%	27%	:	Zone Resistance
100%	80%	58%	60%	29%		:	Zone Support
2%	12%	29%	71%	100%	71%	:	Zone Reached
						:	Zone(5) Close, Zone(6) Open
					50%	:	Zone Resistance
50%	0%	33%	40%	38%	50%	:	Zone Support
12%	12%	19%	31%	50%	100%	:	Zone Reached
						:	Zone(6) Close, Zone(1) Open
50%	40%	0%	0%	33%	0%	:	Zone Resistance
30%						:	Zone Support
100%	50%	30%	30%	30%	20%	:	Zone Reached
						:	Zone(6) Close, Zone(2) Open
	50%	40%	100%			:	Zone Resistance
33%	40%					:	Zone Support
60%	100%	50%	30%	0%	0%	:	Zone Reached
						:	Zone(6) Close, Zone(3) Open
		41%	68%	67%	33%	:	Zone Resistance
20%	69%	48%				:	Zone Support
16%	52%	100%	66%	15%	5%	:	Zone Reached
						:	Zone(6) Close, Zone(4) Open
			56%	61%	39%	:	Zone Resistance
33%	86%	71%	32%			:	Zone Support
3%	20%	68%	100%	44%	17%	:	Zone Reached
						:	Zone(6) Close, Zone(5) Open
				29%	65%	:	Zone Resistance
0%	33%	67%	59%	21%		:	Zone Support
7%	11%	32%	79%	100%	71%	:	Zone Reached
						:	Zone(6) Close, Zone(6) Open
					41%	:	Zone Resistance
0%	43%	30%	17%	43%	38%	:	Zone Support
12%	21%	29%	35%	62%	100%	:	Zone Reached

ZONES (1) - (6)   : ZONE(?) CLOSE, ZONE(?) OPEN

(1)	(2)	(3)	(4)	(5)	(6)		
						:	Zone(1) Close, Zone(1) Open
48%	42%	43%	50%	50%	0%	:	Zone Resistance
39%						:	Zone Support
100%	52%	30%	17%	9%	4%	:	Zone Reached
						:	Zone(1) Close, Zone(2) Open
	12%	66%	62%	80%	0%	:	Zone Resistance
70%	37%					:	Zone Support
63%	100%	88%	30%	12%	2%	:	Zone Reached
						:	Zone(1) Close, Zone(3) Open
		34%	72%	77%	67%	:	Zone Resistance
48%	61%	48%				:	Zone Support
20%	52%	100%	67%	18%	4%	:	Zone Reached
						:	Zone(1) Close, Zone(4) Open
			36%	80%	43%	:	Zone Resistance
40%	41%	60%	24%			:	Zone Support
18%	31%	76%	100%	64%	13%	:	Zone Reached
						:	Zone(1) Close, Zone(5) Open
				43%	0%	:	Zone Resistance
0%	0%	50%	71%	0%		:	Zone Support
14%	14%	29%	100%	100%	57%	:	Zone Reached
						:	Zone(1) Close, Zone(6) Open
					67%	:	Zone Resistance
			100%	0%	67%	:	Zone Support
0%	0%	0%	33%	33%	100%	:	Zone Reached
						:	Zone(2) Close, Zone(1) Open
36%	44%	40%	17%	20%	25%	:	Zone Resistance
39%						:	Zone Support
100%	64%	36%	21%	18%	14%	:	Zone Reached
						:	Zone(2) Close, Zone(2) Open
	22%	68%	38%	80%	100%	:	Zone Resistance
58%	25%					:	Zone Support
75%	100%	78%	25%	16%	3%	:	Zone Reached
						:	Zone(2) Close, Zone(3) Open
		44%	41%	76%	62%	:	Zone Resistance
36%	60%	40%				:	Zone Support
24%	60%	100%	56%	33%	8%	:	Zone Reached
						:	Zone(2) Close, Zone(4) Open
			24%	66%	33%	:	Zone Resistance
33%	45%	68%	26%			:	Zone Support
13%	24%	74%	100%	76%	26%	:	Zone Reached
						:	Zone(2) Close, Zone(5) Open
				12%	33%	:	Zone Resistance
33%	0%	25%	60%	41%		:	Zone Support
18%	18%	24%	59%	100%	88%	:	Zone Reached
						:	Zone(2) Close, Zone(6) Open
					0%	:	Zone Resistance
				100%	20%	:	Zone Support
0%	0%	0%	0%	80%	100%	:	Zone Reached
						:	Zone(3) Close, Zone(1) Open
36%	39%	64%	0%	50%	50%	:	Zone Resistance
50%						:	Zone Support
100%	64%	39%	14%	14%	7%	:	Zone Reached
						:	Zone(3) Close, Zone(2) Open
	27%	60%	25%	50%	17%	:	Zone Resistance
33%	35%					:	Zone Support
65%	100%	73%	29%	22%	11%	:	Zone Reached
						:	Zone(3) Close, Zone(3) Open
		34%	52%	75%	67%	:	Zone Resistance
32%	68%	43%				:	Zone Support
18%	57%	100%	66%	31%	8%	:	Zone Reached
						:	Zone(3) Close, Zone(4) Open
			30%	55%	41%	:	Zone Resistance
40%	48%	60%	38%			:	Zone Support
13%	25%	62%	100%	70%	32%	:	Zone Reached
						:	Zone(3) Close, Zone(5) Open
				30%	37%	:	Zone Resistance
50%	50%	50%	52%	23%		:	Zone Support
9%	19%	37%	77%	100%	70%	:	Zone Reached
						:	Zone(3) Close, Zone(6) Open
					50%	:	Zone Resistance
	100%	75%	20%	29%	50%	:	Zone Support
0%	7%	29%	36%	50%	100%	:	Zone Reached

```
         Z O N E S   (1) - (6)            : ZONE(?) CLOSE, ZONE(?) OPEN


         (1)    (2)    (3)    (4)    (5)    (6)
        ------------------------------------------ : Zone(4) Close, Zone(1) Open
         37%    42%    57%    33%     0%   100%   :     Zone Resistance
         37%                                      :     Zone Support
        100%    63%    37%    16%    11%    11%   :     Zone Reached
        ------------------------------------------ : Zone(4) Close, Zone(2) Open
                31%    56%    38%    43%     0%   :     Zone Resistance
         33%    38%                               :     Zone Support
         62%   100%    69%    33%    18%    10%   :     Zone Reached
        ------------------------------------------ : Zone(4) Close, Zone(3) Open
                       30%    75%    65%    44%   :     Zone Resistance
         23%    69%    35%                        :     Zone Support
         20%    65%   100%    71%    17%     6%   :     Zone Reached
        ------------------------------------------ : Zone(4) Close, Zone(4) Open
                              34%    57%    51%   :     Zone Resistance
         33%    76%    63%    44%                 :     Zone Support
          5%    21%    56%   100%    66%    29%   :     Zone Reached
        ------------------------------------------ : Zone(4) Close, Zone(5) Open
                              33%    26%          :     Zone Resistance
         50%    60%    55%    68%    35%          :     Zone Support
          4%    10%    21%    65%   100%    67%   :     Zone Reached
        ------------------------------------------ : Zone(4) Close, Zone(6) Open
                                            43%   :     Zone Resistance
        100%     0%    67%    25%    73%    50%   :     Zone Support
          3%     3%    10%    13%    50%   100%   :     Zone Reached
        ------------------------------------------ : Zone(5) Close, Zone(1) Open
         67%    50%     0%     0%   100%          :     Zone Resistance
         17%                                      :     Zone Support
        100%    33%    17%    17%    17%     0%   :     Zone Reached
        ------------------------------------------ : Zone(5) Close, Zone(2) Open
                30%    57%    67%    50%   100%   :     Zone Resistance
         31%    20%                               :     Zone Support
         80%   100%    70%    30%    10%     5%   :     Zone Reached
        ------------------------------------------ : Zone(5) Close, Zone(3) Open
                       21%    60%    33%    50%   :     Zone Resistance
         33%    65%    32%                        :     Zone Support
         24%    68%   100%    79%    32%    21%   :     Zone Reached
        ------------------------------------------ : Zone(5) Close, Zone(4) Open
                              41%    72%    50%   :     Zone Resistance
         44%    75%    56%    39%                 :     Zone Support
          7%    27%    61%   100%    59%    16%   :     Zone Reached
        ------------------------------------------ : Zone(5) Close, Zone(5) Open
                              18%    34%          :     Zone Resistance
                100%    50%    67%    38%          :     Zone Support
          0%    10%    21%    62%   100%    82%   :     Zone Reached
        ------------------------------------------ : Zone(5) Close, Zone(6) Open
                                            43%   :     Zone Resistance
                       100%    57%    42%    43%   :     Zone Support
          0%     0%    14%    33%    57%   100%   :     Zone Reached
        ------------------------------------------ : Zone(6) Close, Zone(1) Open
        100%                                      :     Zone Resistance
          0%                                      :     Zone Support
        100%     0%     0%     0%     0%     0%   :     Zone Reached
        ------------------------------------------ : Zone(6) Close, Zone(2) Open
                46%    29%    80%   100%          :     Zone Resistance
         33%    31%                               :     Zone Support
         69%   100%    54%    38%     8%     0%   :     Zone Reached
        ------------------------------------------ : Zone(6) Close, Zone(3) Open
                       30%    67%    55%     0%   :     Zone Resistance
         29%    73%    45%                        :     Zone Support
         15%    55%   100%    70%    23%    11%   :     Zone Reached
        ------------------------------------------ : Zone(6) Close, Zone(4) Open
                              45%    74%    55%   :     Zone Resistance
         57%    82%    59%    36%                 :     Zone Support
          5%    26%    64%   100%    55%    14%   :     Zone Reached
        ------------------------------------------ : Zone(6) Close, Zone(5) Open
                              45%    52%          :     Zone Resistance
         50%    67%    33%    45%    21%          :     Zone Support
         10%    29%    43%    79%   100%    55%   :     Zone Reached
        ------------------------------------------ : Zone(6) Close, Zone(6) Open
                                            55%   :     Zone Resistance
        100%    50%    50%    50%    47%    32%   :     Zone Support
          5%     9%    18%    36%    68%   100%   :     Zone Reached
```

Z O N E S (1) - (6)   : ZONE(?) CLOSE, ZONE(?) OPEN

(1)	(2)	(3)	(4)	(5)	(6)		
						:	Zone(1) Close, Zone(1) Open
35%	35%	54%	27%	50%	25%	:	Zone Resistance
44%						:	Zone Support
100%	65%	42%	19%	14%	7%	:	Zone Reached
						:	Zone(1) Close, Zone(2) Open
	21%	57%	44%	57%	100%	:	Zone Resistance
49%	41%					:	Zone Support
60%	97%	77%	35%	18%	8%	:	Zone Reached
						:	Zone(1) Close, Zone(3) Open
		34%	55%	80%	58%	:	Zone Resistance
58%	70%	46%				:	Zone Support
16%	54%	100%	66%	29%	6%	:	Zone Reached
						:	Zone(1) Close, Zone(4) Open
			53%	57%	31%	:	Zone Resistance
33%	65%	69%	16%			:	Zone Support
9%	27%	84%	100%	47%	20%	:	Zone Reached
						:	Zone(1) Close, Zone(5) Open
				46%	21%	:	Zone Resistance
50%	56%	31%	32%	27%		:	Zone Support
15%	35%	50%	73%	100%	54%	:	Zone Reached
						:	Zone(1) Close, Zone(6) Open
					56%	:	Zone Resistance
75%	20%	0%	29%	12%	11%	:	Zone Support
44%	56%	56%	78%	89%	100%	:	Zone Reached
						:	Zone(2) Close, Zone(1) Open
44%	53%	33%	50%	33%	50%	:	Zone Resistance
32%						:	Zone Support
100%	56%	26%	18%	9%	6%	:	Zone Reached
						:	Zone(2) Close, Zone(2) Open
	31%	32%	64%	56%	100%	:	Zone Resistance
43%	35%					:	Zone Support
65%	100%	69%	46%	17%	7%	:	Zone Reached
						:	Zone(2) Close, Zone(3) Open
		31%	60%	63%	15%	:	Zone Resistance
39%	68%	44%				:	Zone Support
18%	56%	100%	69%	27%	10%	:	Zone Reached
						:	Zone(2) Close, Zone(4) Open
			37%	62%	53%	:	Zone Resistance
42%	40%	55%	30%			:	Zone Support
19%	32%	70%	100%	63%	24%	:	Zone Reached
						:	Zone(2) Close, Zone(5) Open
				41%	29%	:	Zone Resistance
50%	71%	30%	50%	31%		:	Zone Support
7%	24%	34%	69%	100%	59%	:	Zone Reached
						:	Zone(2) Close, Zone(6) Open
					38%	:	Zone Resistance
		100%	50%	67%	25%	:	Zone Support
0%	0%	12%	25%	75%	100%	:	Zone Reached
						:	Zone(3) Close, Zone(1) Open
54%	61%	57%	100%			:	Zone Resistance
36%						:	Zone Support
100%	46%	18%	8%	0%	0%	:	Zone Reached
						:	Zone(3) Close, Zone(2) Open
	38%	64%	44%	50%	75%	:	Zone Resistance
35%	25%					:	Zone Support
75%	100%	62%	25%	11%	5%	:	Zone Reached
						:	Zone(3) Close, Zone(3) Open
		36%	60%	69%	13%	:	Zone Resistance
43%	58%	41%				:	Zone Support
24%	59%	100%	64%	25%	8%	:	Zone Reached
						:	Zone(3) Close, Zone(4) Open
			31%	55%	57%	:	Zone Resistance
38%	59%	62%	40%			:	Zone Support
9%	23%	60%	100%	69%	31%	:	Zone Reached
						:	Zone(3) Close, Zone(5) Open
				34%	51%	:	Zone Resistance
50%	71%	63%	61%	25%		:	Zone Support
3%	11%	29%	75%	100%	66%	:	Zone Reached
						:	Zone(3) Close, Zone(6) Open
					34%	:	Zone Resistance
50%	0%	0%	33%	75%	59%	:	Zone Support
7%	7%	7%	10%	41%	100%	:	Zone Reached

Z O N E S   (1) - (6)   : ZONE(?) CLOSE, ZONE(?) OPEN

(1)	(2)	(3)	(4)	(5)	(6)	
						: Zone(4) Close, Zone(1) Open
48%	50%	86%	100%			: Zone Resistance
33%						: Zone Support
100%	52%	26%	4%	0%	0%	: Zone Reached
						: Zone(4) Close, Zone(2) Open
	27%	65%	63%	71%	0%	: Zone Resistance
33%	39%					: Zone Support
61%	100%	73%	26%	9%	3%	: Zone Reached
						: Zone(4) Close, Zone(3) Open
		32%	56%	63%	27%	: Zone Resistance
47%	63%	36%				: Zone Support
24%	64%	100%	68%	30%	11%	: Zone Reached
						: Zone(4) Close, Zone(4) Open
			38%	58%	27%	: Zone Resistance
40%	72%	61%	38%			: Zone Support
7%	24%	62%	100%	62%	26%	: Zone Reached
						: Zone(4) Close, Zone(5) Open
				30%	30%	: Zone Resistance
17%	50%	25%	72%	34%		: Zone Support
7%	14%	18%	66%	100%	70%	: Zone Reached
						: Zone(4) Close, Zone(6) Open
					34%	: Zone Resistance
0%	20%	17%	33%	65%	32%	: Zone Support
11%	13%	16%	24%	68%	100%	: Zone Reached
						: Zone(5) Close, Zone(1) Open
29%	50%	60%	50%	100%		: Zone Resistance
29%						: Zone Support
100%	71%	36%	14%	7%	0%	: Zone Reached
						: Zone(5) Close, Zone(2) Open
	32%	48%	36%	43%	75%	: Zone Resistance
52%	26%					: Zone Support
74%	100%	68%	35%	23%	13%	: Zone Reached
						: Zone(5) Close, Zone(3) Open
		34%	72%	55%	40%	: Zone Resistance
44%	61%	33%				: Zone Support
26%	67%	100%	66%	18%	8%	: Zone Reached
						: Zone(5) Close, Zone(4) Open
			39%	62%	37%	: Zone Resistance
57%	60%	62%	40%			: Zone Support
9%	23%	60%	100%	61%	23%	: Zone Reached
						: Zone(5) Close, Zone(5) Open
				38%	44%	: Zone Resistance
67%	67%	47%	64%	19%		: Zone Support
5%	16%	29%	81%	100%	62%	: Zone Reached
						: Zone(5) Close, Zone(6) Open
					48%	: Zone Resistance
100%	0%	75%	47%	42%	38%	: Zone Support
5%	5%	19%	36%	62%	100%	: Zone Reached
						: Zone(6) Close, Zone(1) Open
50%	0%	25%	100%			: Zone Resistance
38%						: Zone Support
100%	50%	50%	38%	0%	0%	: Zone Reached
						: Zone(6) Close, Zone(2) Open
	27%	47%	40%	17%	20%	: Zone Resistance
33%	42%					: Zone Support
58%	100%	73%	38%	23%	19%	: Zone Reached
						: Zone(6) Close, Zone(3) Open
		31%	75%	43%	0%	: Zone Resistance
67%	72%	33%				: Zone Support
19%	67%	100%	69%	17%	10%	: Zone Reached
						: Zone(6) Close, Zone(4) Open
			44%	63%	56%	: Zone Resistance
23%	68%	66%	38%			: Zone Support
7%	21%	62%	100%	56%	21%	: Zone Reached
						: Zone(6) Close, Zone(5) Open
				38%	69%	: Zone Resistance
33%	77%	50%	59%	7%		: Zone Support
4%	19%	38%	93%	100%	62%	: Zone Reached
						: Zone(6) Close, Zone(6) Open
					60%	: Zone Resistance
67%	33%	10%	55%	24%	38%	: Zone Support
13%	19%	21%	47%	62%	100%	: Zone Reached

*** UNLEADED GASOLINE ***

Z O N E S (1) - (6)   : ZONE(?) CLOSE, ZONE(?) OPEN

(1)	(2)	(3)	(4)	(5)	(6)		
						:	Zone(1) Close, Zone(1) Open
37%	35%	55%	0%	80%	0%	:	Zone Resistance
56%						:	Zone Support
100%	63%	41%	19%	19%	4%	:	Zone Reached
						:	Zone(1) Close, Zone(2) Open
	21%	57%	60%	50%	100%	:	Zone Resistance
42%	34%					:	Zone Support
66%	100%	79%	34%	14%	7%	:	Zone Reached
						:	Zone(1) Close, Zone(3) Open
.		43%	55%	83%	20%	:	Zone Resistance
39%	54%	46%				:	Zone Support
25%	54%	100%	58%	25%	4%	:	Zone Reached
						:	Zone(1) Close, Zone(4) Open
			52%	65%	43%	:	Zone Resistance
60%	55%	65%	26%			:	Zone Support
12%	26%	74%	100%	48%	17%	:	Zone Reached
						:	Zone(1) Close, Zone(5) Open
				56%	25%	:	Zone Resistance
100%	67%	25%	43%	22%		:	Zone Support
11%	33%	44%	78%	100%	44%	:	Zone Reached
						:	Zone(1) Close, Zone(6) Open
					0%	:	Zone Resistance
		100%	0%	67%	40%	:	Zone Support
0%	0%	20%	20%	60%	100%	:	Zone Reached
						:	Zone(2) Close, Zone(1) Open
40%	50%	33%	50%	100%		:	Zone Resistance
45%						:	Zone Support
100%	60%	30%	20%	10%	0%	:	Zone Reached
						:	Zone(2) Close, Zone(2) Open
	34%	42%	36%	43%	25%	:	Zone Resistance
45%	31%					:	Zone Support
69%	100%	66%	38%	24%	14%	:	Zone Reached
						:	Zone(2) Close, Zone(3) Open
		37%	57%	71%	40%	:	Zone Resistance
50%	69%	38%				:	Zone Support
19%	62%	100%	63%	27%	8%	:	Zone Reached
						:	Zone(2) Close, Zone(4) Open
			36%	52%	64%	:	Zone Resistance
50%	50%	61%	14%			:	Zone Support
17%	33%	86%	100%	64%	31%	:	Zone Reached
						:	Zone(2) Close, Zone(5) Open
				47%	56%	:	Zone Resistance
0%	50%	56%	40%	12%		:	Zone Support
12%	24%	53%	88%	100%	53%	:	Zone Reached
						:	Zone(2) Close, Zone(6) Open
					33%	:	Zone Resistance
		100%	0%	80%	44%	:	Zone Support
0%	0%	11%	11%	56%	100%	:	Zone Reached
						:	Zone(3) Close, Zone(1) Open
24%	32%	60%	50%	0%	33%	:	Zone Resistance
66%						:	Zone Support
100%	76%	52%	21%	10%	10%	:	Zone Reached
						:	Zone(3) Close, Zone(2) Open
	24%	68%	44%	40%	33%	:	Zone Resistance
32%	41%					:	Zone Support
59%	100%	76%	24%	14%	8%	:	Zone Reached
						:	Zone(3) Close, Zone(3) Open
		42%	52%	64%	33%	:	Zone Resistance
38%	53%	43%				:	Zone Support
27%	57%	100%	58%	28%	10%	:	Zone Reached
						:	Zone(3) Close, Zone(4) Open
			38%	50%	48%	:	Zone Resistance
50%	58%	64%	38%			:	Zone Support
9%	22%	61%	99%	62%	31%	:	Zone Reached
						:	Zone(3) Close, Zone(5) Open
				39%	45%	:	Zone Resistance
0%	40%	38%	70%	18%		:	Zone Support
9%	15%	24%	82%	100%	61%	:	Zone Reached
						:	Zone(3) Close, Zone(6) Open
					47%	:	Zone Resistance
0%	0%	50%	60%	44%	53%	:	Zone Support
5%	5%	11%	26%	47%	100%	:	Zone Reached

```
Z O N E S   (1) - (6)              : ZONE(?) CLOSE, ZONE(?) OPEN


        (1)    (2)    (3)    (4)    (5)    (6)
--------------------------------------------------- : Zone(4) Close, Zone(1) Open
        32%    33%    50%    80%     0%     0%       :   Zone Resistance
        45%                                          :   Zone Support
       100%    68%    45%    23%     5%     5%   :   Zone Reached
--------------------------------------------------- : Zone(4) Close, Zone(2) Open
               30%    57%    50%    40%    33%   :   Zone Resistance
        33%    36%                               :   Zone Support
        64%   100%    70%    30%    15%     9%   :   Zone Support
--------------------------------------------------- : Zone(4) Close, Zone(3) Open
                      30%    62%    63%    60%   :   Zone Resistance
        50%    64%    36%                         :   Zone Support
        23%    64%   100%    70%    26%    10%   :   Zone Reached
--------------------------------------------------- : Zone(4) Close, Zone(4) Open
                             34%    46%    44%   :   Zone Resistance
        30%    67%    62%    34%                 :   Zone Support
         8%    25%    66%   100%    66%    36%   :   Zone Reached
--------------------------------------------------- : Zone(4) Close, Zone(5) Open
                                    39%    22%   :   Zone Resistance
         0%    71%    30%    55%    42%          :   Zone Support
         5%    18%    26%    58%   100%    61%   :   Zone Reached
--------------------------------------------------- : Zone(4) Close, Zone(6) Open
                                           45%   :   Zone Resistance
       100%    50%    60%    44%    53%    42%   :   Zone Support
         3%     6%    15%    27%    58%   100%   :   Zone Reached
--------------------------------------------------- : Zone(5) Close, Zone(1) Open
        67%     0%     0%   100%                 :   Zone Resistance
        67%                                       :   Zone Support
       100%    33%    33%    33%     0%     0%   :   Zone Reached
--------------------------------------------------- : Zone(5) Close, Zone(2) Open
               33%    50%    50%    75%     0%   :   Zone Resistance
        53%    21%                               :   Zone Support
        79%   100%    67%    33%    17%     4%   :   Zone Reached
--------------------------------------------------- : Zone(5) Close, Zone(3) Open
                      23%    70%    50%    25%   :   Zone Resistance
        62%    58%    46%                         :   Zone Support
        23%    54%   100%    77%    23%    11%   :   Zone Reached
--------------------------------------------------- : Zone(5) Close, Zone(4) Open
                             31%    66%    50%   :   Zone Resistance
        44%    53%    58%    46%                 :   Zone Support
        11%    23%    54%   100%    69%    24%   :   Zone Reached
--------------------------------------------------- : Zone(5) Close, Zone(5) Open
                                    32%    46%   :   Zone Resistance
        50%    67%    57%    36%    42%          :   Zone Support
         5%    16%    37%    58%   100%    68%   :   Zone Reached
--------------------------------------------------- : Zone(5) Close, Zone(6) Open
                                           36%   :   Zone Resistance
        33%     0%    25%    56%    10%    60%   :   Zone Support
        12%    12%    16%    36%    40%   100%   :   Zone Reached
--------------------------------------------------- : Zone(6) Close, Zone(1) Open
        57%     0%    33%    50%     0%     0%   :   Zone Resistance
        43%                                       :   Zone Support
       100%    43%    43%    29%    14%    14%   :   Zone Reached
--------------------------------------------------- : Zone(6) Close, Zone(2) Open
               17%    47%    25%    50%    33%   :   Zone Resistance
        36%    39%                               :   Zone Support
        61%   100%    83%    44%    33%    17%   :   Zone Reached
--------------------------------------------------- : Zone(6) Close, Zone(3) Open
                      22%    61%    73%    67%   :   Zone Resistance
        67%    74%    36%                         :   Zone Support
        17%    64%   100%    78%    31%     8%   :   Zone Reached
--------------------------------------------------- : Zone(6) Close, Zone(4) Open
                             48%    58%    36%   :   Zone Resistance
        40%    76%    66%    47%                 :   Zone Support
         4%    18%    53%   100%    52%    22%   :   Zone Reached
--------------------------------------------------- : Zone(6) Close, Zone(5) Open
                                    42%    65%   :   Zone Resistance
        50%    20%    55%    68%    24%          :   Zone Support
         9%    11%    24%    76%   100%    58%   :   Zone Reached
--------------------------------------------------- : Zone(6) Close, Zone(6) Open
                                           72%   :   Zone Resistance
         0%    67%    67%    44%    24%    34%   :   Zone Support
         3%     9%    28%    50%    66%   100%   :   Zone Reached
```

```
                        *** GOLD ***


        Z O N E S  (1) - (6)        : ZONE(?) CLOSE, ZONE(?) OPEN


       (1)    (2)    (3)    (4)    (5)    (6)
    ---------------------------------------------- : Zone(1) Close, Zone(1) Open
       45%    44%    44%    40%    67%   100%   :    Zone Resistance
       52%                                      :    Zone Support
      100%    55%    31%    17%    10%     3%   :    Zone Reached
    ---------------------------------------------- : Zone(1) Close, Zone(2) Open
               6%    62%    71%   100%          :    Zone Resistance
       62%    46%                               :    Zone Support
       54%   100%    94%    35%    10%     0%   :    Zone Reached
    ---------------------------------------------- : Zone(1) Close, Zone(3) Open
                     39%    72%    77%    50%   :    Zone Resistance
       58%    62%    59%                        :    Zone Support
       15%    41%   100%    62%    16%     4%   :    Zone Reached
    ---------------------------------------------- : Zone(1) Close, Zone(4) Open
                            54%    60%    33%   :    Zone Resistance
       50%    47%    68%    28%                 :    Zone Support
       12%    23%    72%   100%    46%    18%   :    Zone Reached
    ---------------------------------------------- : Zone(1) Close, Zone(5) Open
                                   47%    38%   :    Zone Resistance
              100%    67%    75%    20%         :    Zone Support
        0%     7%    20%    80%   100%    53%   :    Zone Reached
    ---------------------------------------------- : Zone(1) Close, Zone(6) Open
                                          25%   :    Zone Resistance
                            100%    67%    25%  :    Zone Support
        0%     0%     0%    25%    75%   100%   :    Zone Reached
    ---------------------------------------------- : Zone(2) Close, Zone(1) Open
       24%    58%    38%   100%                 :    Zone Resistance
       48%                                      :    Zone Support
      100%    76%    32%    20%     0%     0%   :    Zone Reached
    ---------------------------------------------- : Zone(2) Close, Zone(2) Open
              29%    33%    56%    57%    67%   :    Zone Resistance
       30%    41%                               :    Zone Support
       59%   100%    71%    47%    21%     9%   :    Zone Reached
    ---------------------------------------------- : Zone(2) Close, Zone(3) Open
                     28%    59%    68%    54%   :    Zone Resistance
       42%    60%    57%                        :    Zone Support
       17%    43%   100%    72%    29%     9%   :    Zone Reached
    ---------------------------------------------- : Zone(2) Close, Zone(4) Open
                            40%    60%    29%   :    Zone Resistance
       50%    50%    76%    30%                 :    Zone Support
        9%    17%    70%   100%    60%    24%   :    Zone Reached
    ---------------------------------------------- : Zone(2) Close, Zone(5) Open
                                   53%    62%   :    Zone Resistance
       33%     0%    50%    54%    24%          :    Zone Support
       18%    18%    35%    76%   100%    47%   :    Zone Reached
    ---------------------------------------------- : Zone(2) Close, Zone(6) Open
                                          71%   :    Zone Resistance
      100%     0%    33%    40%     0%    29%   :    Zone Support
       29%    29%    43%    71%    71%   100%   :    Zone Reached
    ---------------------------------------------- : Zone(3) Close, Zone(1) Open
       28%    54%    32%    33%    50%    50%   :    Zone Resistance
       51%                                      :    Zone Support
      100%    72%    33%    26%    14%     7%   :    Zone Reached
    ---------------------------------------------- : Zone(3) Close, Zone(2) Open
              25%    55%    50%    50%    67%   :    Zone Resistance
       47%    25%                               :    Zone Support
       75%   100%    75%    36%    16%     8%   :    Zone Reached
    ---------------------------------------------- : Zone(3) Close, Zone(3) Open
                     25%    58%    62%    36%   :    Zone Resistance
       58%    52%    45%                        :    Zone Support
       26%    55%   100%    75%    31%    12%   :    Zone Reached
    ---------------------------------------------- : Zone(3) Close, Zone(4) Open
                            36%    58%    48%   :    Zone Resistance
       43%    50%    66%    29%                 :    Zone Support
       12%    24%    71%   100%    64%    27%   :    Zone Reached
    ---------------------------------------------- : Zone(3) Close, Zone(5) Open
                                   36%    55%   :    Zone Resistance
       33%    25%    29%    50%    24%          :    Zone Support
       20%    27%    38%    76%   100%    64%   :    Zone Reached
    ---------------------------------------------- : Zone(3) Close, Zone(6) Open
                                          44%   :    Zone Resistance
       50%    33%    50%    54%    43%    32%   :    Zone Support
        6%     9%    18%    38%    68%   100%   :    Zone Reached
```

ZONES (1) - (6)   : ZONE(?) CLOSE, ZONE(?) OPEN

(1)	(2)	(3)	(4)	(5)	(6)		
						:	Zone(4) Close, Zone(1) Open
43%	42%	60%	17%	60%	50%	:	Zone Resistance
43%						:	Zone Support
100%	57%	33%	13%	11%	4%	:	Zone Reached
						:	Zone(4) Close, Zone(2) Open
	22%	57%	55%	67%	33%	:	Zone Resistance
58%	39%					:	Zone Support
61%	100%	78%	34%	15%	5%	:	Zone Reached
						:	Zone(4) Close, Zone(3) Open
		25%	61%	53%	53%	:	Zone Resistance
57%	58%	37%				:	Zone Support
27%	63%	100%	76%	28%	13%	:	Zone Reached
						:	Zone(4) Close, Zone(4) Open
			44%	55%	48%	:	Zone Resistance
53%	66%	56%	26%			:	Zone Support
11%	33%	74%	100%	56%	25%	:	Zone Reached
						:	Zone(4) Close, Zone(5) Open
				35%	57%	:	Zone Resistance
38%	50%	59%	40%	22%		:	Zone Support
10%	19%	47%	78%	100%	65%	:	Zone Reached
						:	Zone(4) Close, Zone(6) Open
					56%	:	Zone Resistance
0%	50%	33%	53%	46%	36%	:	Zone Support
5%	11%	16%	35%	64%	100%	:	Zone Reached
						:	Zone(5) Close, Zone(1) Open
50%	22%	86%	0%	100%		:	Zone Resistance
56%						:	Zone Support
100%	50%	39%	6%	6%	0%	:	Zone Reached
						:	Zone(5) Close, Zone(2) Open
	19%	52%	80%	50%	0%	:	Zone Resistance
61%	31%					:	Zone Support
69%	100%	81%	38%	8%	4%	:	Zone Reached
						:	Zone(5) Close, Zone(3) Open
		34%	65%	62%	33%	:	Zone Resistance
47%	58%	38%				:	Zone Support
26%	62%	100%	67%	22%	8%	:	Zone Reached
						:	Zone(5) Close, Zone(4) Open
			61%	59%	40%	:	Zone Resistance
64%	70%	53%	22%			:	Zone Support
11%	37%	78%	100%	39%	16%	:	Zone Reached
						:	Zone(5) Close, Zone(5) Open
				39%	59%	:	Zone Resistance
100%	67%	60%	55%	8%		:	Zone Support
6%	17%	42%	92%	100%	61%	:	Zone Reached
						:	Zone(5) Close, Zone(6) Open
					46%	:	Zone Resistance
100%	50%	50%	43%	53%	42%	:	Zone Support
4%	8%	15%	27%	58%	100%	:	Zone Reached
						:	Zone(6) Close, Zone(1) Open
56%	25%	33%	0%	0%	50%	:	Zone Resistance
33%						:	Zone Support
100%	44%	33%	22%	22%	22%	:	Zone Reached
						:	Zone(6) Close, Zone(2) Open
	28%	62%	88%	0%	0%	:	Zone Resistance
70%	31%					:	Zone Support
69%	100%	72%	28%	3%	3%	:	Zone Reached
						:	Zone(6) Close, Zone(3) Open
		33%	85%	67%	50%	:	Zone Resistance
33%	79%	52%				:	Zone Support
10%	48%	100%	67%	10%	3%	:	Zone Reached
						:	Zone(6) Close, Zone(4) Open
			64%	53%	53%	:	Zone Resistance
33%	72%	66%	30%			:	Zone Support
7%	24%	70%	100%	36%	17%	:	Zone Reached
						:	Zone(6) Close, Zone(5) Open
				38%	67%	:	Zone Resistance
	100%	33%	55%	17%		:	Zone Support
0%	25%	38%	83%	100%	62%	:	Zone Reached
						:	Zone(6) Close, Zone(6) Open
					65%	:	Zone Resistance
50%	67%	25%	38%	24%	45%	:	Zone Support
6%	19%	26%	42%	55%	100%	:	Zone Reached

```
                      *** SILVER ***


        Z O N E S  (1) - (6)          : ZONE(?) CLOSE, ZONE(?) OPEN


       (1)    (2)    (3)    (4)    (5)    (6)
      ------------------------------------------ : Zone(1) Close, Zone(1) Open
       71%    32%    69%    50%    50%    0%   :    Zone Resistance
       28%                                     :    Zone Support
      100%    29%    20%    6%     3%     2%   :    Zone Reached
      ------------------------------------------ : Zone(1) Close, Zone(2) Open
              16%    66%    36%    86%    0%   :    Zone Resistance
       42%    37%                              :    Zone Support
       63%   100%    84%    29%    18%    3%   :    Zone Reached
      ------------------------------------------ : Zone(1) Close, Zone(3) Open
                     48%    65%    82%    57%  :    Zone Resistance
       39%    56%    50%                       :    Zone Support
       22%    50%   100%    54%    17%    3%   :    Zone Reached
      ------------------------------------------ : Zone(1) Close, Zone(4) Open
                            45%    64%    38%  :    Zone Resistance
       50%    33%    83%    18%                :    Zone Support
       9%     14%    82%   100%    55%    20%  :    Zone Reached
      ------------------------------------------ : Zone(1) Close, Zone(5) Open
                                   32%    46%  :    Zone Resistance
       75%    20%    44%    36%    26%         :    Zone Support
       21%    26%    47%    74%   100%    68%  :    Zone Reached
      ------------------------------------------ : Zone(1) Close, Zone(6) Open
                                          60%  :    Zone Resistance
       50%    0%     20%    17%    14%    30%  :    Zone Support
       40%    40%    50%    60%    70%   100%  :    Zone Reached
      ------------------------------------------ : Zone(2) Close, Zone(1) Open
       40%    47%    62%    33%    50%   100%  :    Zone Resistance
       40%                                     :    Zone Support
      100%    60%    32%    12%    8%     4%   :    Zone Reached
      ------------------------------------------ : Zone(2) Close, Zone(2) Open
              17%    40%    33%    75%    50%  :    Zone Resistance
       57%    42%                              :    Zone Support
       58%   100%    83%    50%    33%    8%   :    Zone Reached
      ------------------------------------------ : Zone(2) Close, Zone(3) Open
                     33%    65%    67%    73%  :    Zone Resistance
       42%    57%    60%                       :    Zone Support
       17%    40%   100%    67%    24%    8%   :    Zone Reached
      ------------------------------------------ : Zone(2) Close, Zone(4) Open
                            49%    69%    36%  :    Zone Resistance
       23%    24%    71%    18%                :    Zone Support
       18%    24%    82%   100%    51%    15%  :    Zone Reached
      ------------------------------------------ : Zone(2) Close, Zone(5) Open
                                   39%    55%  :    Zone Resistance
       50%    0%     60%    55%    39%         :    Zone Support
       11%    11%    28%    61%   100%    61%  :    Zone Reached
      ------------------------------------------ : Zone(2) Close, Zone(6) Open
                                          0%   :    Zone Resistance
                            100%    67%    25%  :    Zone Support
       0%     0%     0%     25%    75%   100%  :    Zone Reached
      ------------------------------------------ : Zone(3) Close, Zone(1) Open
       40%    45%    69%    20%    75%    0%   :    Zone Resistance
       40%                                     :    Zone Support
      100%    60%    33%    10%    8%     2%   :    Zone Reached
      ------------------------------------------ : Zone(3) Close, Zone(2) Open
              12%    39%    49%    50%    60%  :    Zone Resistance
       49%    35%                              :    Zone Support
       65%   100%    88%    55%    27%    13%  :    Zone Reached
      ------------------------------------------ : Zone(3) Close, Zone(3) Open
                     19%    60%    63%    59%  :    Zone Resistance
       36%    54%    49%                       :    Zone Support
       23%    51%   100%    82%    32%    12%  :    Zone Reached
      ------------------------------------------ : Zone(3) Close, Zone(4) Open
                            32%    67%    38%  :    Zone Resistance
       35%    44%    66%    28%                :    Zone Support
       14%    24%    71%   100%    68%    22%  :    Zone Reached
      ------------------------------------------ : Zone(3) Close, Zone(5) Open
                                   40%    56%  :    Zone Resistance
       67%    50%    56%    43%    18%         :    Zone Support
       11%    21%    47%    82%   100%    60%  :    Zone Reached
      ------------------------------------------ : Zone(3) Close, Zone(6) Open
                                          50%  :    Zone Resistance
       50%    0%     50%    43%    36%    8%   :    Zone Support
       17%    17%    33%    58%    92%   100%  :    Zone Reached
```

ZONES (1) - (6)   : ZONE(?) CLOSE, ZONE(?) OPEN

(1)	(2)	(3)	(4)	(5)	(6)		
						:	Zone(4) Close, Zone(1) Open
44%	53%	22%	14%	50%	33%	:	Zone Resistance
29%						:	Zone Support
100%	56%	26%	21%	18%	9%	:	Zone Reached
						:	Zone(4) Close, Zone(2) Open
	28%	46%	43%	44%	56%	:	Zone Resistance
49%	38%					:	Zone Support
62%	100%	72%	39%	22%	12%	:	Zone Reached
						:	Zone(4) Close, Zone(3) Open
		26%	61%	55%	40%	:	Zone Resistance
48%	61%	42%				:	Zone Support
23%	58%	100%	75%	27%	12%	:	Zone Reached
						:	Zone(4) Close, Zone(4) Open
			37%	54%	47%	:	Zone Resistance
57%	57%	64%	28%			:	Zone Support
11%	25%	72%	99%	63%	29%	:	Zone Reached
						:	Zone(4) Close, Zone(5) Open
				42%	55%	:	Zone Resistance
38%	60%	39%	44%	22%		:	Zone Support
11%	26%	43%	78%	100%	58%	:	Zone Reached
						:	Zone(4) Close, Zone(6) Open
					52%	:	Zone Resistance
50%	33%	62%	50%	33%	40%	:	Zone Support
5%	8%	20%	40%	60%	100%	:	Zone Reached
						:	Zone(5) Close, Zone(1) Open
22%	43%	25%	67%	0%	0%	:	Zone Resistance
67%						:	Zone Support
100%	78%	44%	33%	11%	11%	:	Zone Reached
						:	Zone(5) Close, Zone(2) Open
	18%	65%	44%	50%	50%	:	Zone Resistance
38%	54%					:	Zone Support
46%	100%	82%	32%	14%	7%	:	Zone Reached
						:	Zone(5) Close, Zone(3) Open
		19%	73%	50%	62%	:	Zone Resistance
31%	61%	45%				:	Zone Support
21%	55%	100%	83%	21%	11%	:	Zone Reached
						:	Zone(5) Close, Zone(4) Open
			61%	69%	56%	:	Zone Resistance
53%	61%	65%	17%			:	Zone Support
12%	29%	83%	100%	39%	12%	:	Zone Reached
						:	Zone(5) Close, Zone(5) Open
				47%	62%	:	Zone Resistance
0%	67%	50%	57%	7%		:	Zone Support
7%	20%	40%	93%	100%	53%	:	Zone Reached
						:	Zone(5) Close, Zone(6) Open
					23%	:	Zone Resistance
		100%	25%	56%	59%	:	Zone Support
0%	0%	14%	18%	41%	100%	:	Zone Reached
						:	Zone(6) Close, Zone(1) Open
88%	100%					:	Zone Resistance
12%						:	Zone Support
100%	12%	0%	0%	0%	0%	:	Zone Reached
						:	Zone(6) Close, Zone(2) Open
	18%	29%	30%	29%	60%	:	Zone Resistance
56%	47%					:	Zone Support
53%	100%	82%	59%	41%	29%	:	Zone Reached
						:	Zone(6) Close, Zone(3) Open
		21%	76%	50%	20%	:	Zone Resistance
43%	74%	53%				:	Zone Support
12%	47%	100%	81%	18%	9%	:	Zone Reached
						:	Zone(6) Close, Zone(4) Open
			54%	55%	44%	:	Zone Resistance
50%	85%	68%	31%			:	Zone Support
3%	22%	69%	100%	46%	21%	:	Zone Reached
						:	Zone(6) Close, Zone(5) Open
				44%	35%	:	Zone Resistance
67%	40%	71%	43%	17%		:	Zone Support
8%	14%	47%	83%	100%	56%	:	Zone Reached
						:	Zone(6) Close, Zone(6) Open
					48%	:	Zone Resistance
33%	33%	10%	41%	23%	52%	:	Zone Support
13%	20%	22%	37%	48%	100%	:	Zone Reached

```
          Z O N E S  (1) - (6)            : ZONE(?) CLOSE, ZONE(?) OPEN
```

(1)	(2)	(3)	(4)	(5)	(6)		
						:	Zone(1) Close, Zone(1) Open
55%	56%	0%	25%	67%	100%	:	Zone Resistance
30%						:	Zone Support
100%	45%	20%	20%	15%	5%	:	Zone Reached
						:	Zone(1) Close, Zone(2) Open
	10%	51%	61%	43%	0%	:	Zone Resistance
45%	46%					:	Zone Support
54%	100%	90%	44%	17%	10%	:	Zone Reached
						:	Zone(1) Close, Zone(3) Open
		46%	64%	79%	12%	:	Zone Resistance
37%	62%	52%				:	Zone Support
18%	48%	100%	55%	18%	4%	:	Zone Reached
						:	Zone(1) Close, Zone(4) Open
			47%	59%	25%	:	Zone Resistance
100%	67%	77%	29%			:	Zone Support
5%	16%	71%	100%	53%	22%	:	Zone Reached
						:	Zone(1) Close, Zone(5) Open
				43%	31%	:	Zone Resistance
0%	0%	83%	70%	13%		:	Zone Support
4%	4%	26%	87%	100%	57%	:	Zone Reached
						:	Zone(1) Close, Zone(6) Open
					50%	:	Zone Resistance
				100%	50%	:	Zone Support
0%	0%	0%	0%	50%	100%	:	Zone Reached
						:	Zone(2) Close, Zone(1) Open
25%	53%	86%	100%			:	Zone Resistance
25%						:	Zone Support
100%	75%	35%	5%	0%	0%	:	Zone Reached
						:	Zone(2) Close, Zone(2) Open
	13%	56%	53%	57%	0%	:	Zone Resistance
42%	41%					:	Zone Support
60%	98%	85%	38%	18%	8%	:	Zone Reached
						:	Zone(2) Close, Zone(3) Open
		38%	52%	57%	56%	:	Zone Resistance
52%	51%	41%				:	Zone Support
29%	59%	100%	64%	29%	12%	:	Zone Reached
						:	Zone(2) Close, Zone(4) Open
			24%	62%	50%	:	Zone Resistance
38%	47%	71%	32%			:	Zone Support
11%	20%	68%	100%	76%	29%	:	Zone Reached
						:	Zone(2) Close, Zone(5) Open
				27%	31%	:	Zone Resistance
100%	0%	80%	64%	36%		:	Zone Support
5%	5%	23%	64%	100%	73%	:	Zone Reached
						:	Zone(2) Close, Zone(6) Open
					57%	:	Zone Resistance
		100%	67%	50%	14%	:	Zone Support
0%	0%	14%	43%	86%	100%	:	Zone Reached
						:	Zone(3) Close, Zone(1) Open
19%	65%	78%	67%			:	Zone Resistance
47%						:	Zone Support
100%	81%	28%	9%	0%	0%	:	Zone Reached
						:	Zone(3) Close, Zone(2) Open
	19%	67%	53%	57%	0%	:	Zone Resistance
44%	21%					:	Zone Support
79%	100%	81%	26%	12%	5%	:	Zone Reached
						:	Zone(3) Close, Zone(3) Open
		35%	53%	70%	62%	:	Zone Resistance
50%	49%	37%				:	Zone Support
32%	63%	100%	68%	29%	9%	:	Zone Reached
						:	Zone(3) Close, Zone(4) Open
			29%	52%	63%	:	Zone Resistance
45%	51%	64%	34%			:	Zone Support
11%	23%	65%	99%	71%	34%	:	Zone Reached
						:	Zone(3) Close, Zone(5) Open
				18%	42%	:	Zone Resistance
33%	40%	75%	58%	40%		:	Zone Support
4%	6%	25%	60%	100%	82%	:	Zone Reached
						:	Zone(3) Close, Zone(6) Open
					30%	:	Zone Resistance
	100%	67%	50%	50%	40%	:	Zone Support
0%	5%	15%	30%	60%	100%	:	Zone Reached

ZONES (1) - (6)   : ZONE(?) CLOSE, ZONE(?) OPEN

	(1)	(2)	(3)	(4)	(5)	(6)		
							:	Zone(4) Close, Zone(1) Open
Zone Resistance	29%	71%	60%	0%	50%	0%	:	
Zone Support	38%						:	
Zone Reached	100%	71%	21%	8%	8%	4%	:	
							:	Zone(4) Close, Zone(2) Open
Zone Resistance		28%	57%	64%	38%	20%	:	
Zone Support	51%	25%					:	
Zone Reached	75%	100%	72%	31%	11%	7%	:	
							:	Zone(4) Close, Zone(3) Open
Zone Resistance			26%	57%	51%	38%	:	
Zone Support	33%	60%	37%				:	
Zone Reached	25%	63%	100%	74%	32%	16%	:	
							:	Zone(4) Close, Zone(4) Open
Zone Resistance				33%	56%	44%	:	
Zone Support	45%	60%	55%	40%			:	
Zone Reached	11%	27%	59%	100%	67%	29%	:	
							:	Zone(4) Close, Zone(5) Open
Zone Resistance				28%	46%		:	
Zone Support	67%	45%	50%	48%	22%		:	
Zone Reached	11%	20%	41%	78%	100%	72%	:	
							:	Zone(4) Close, Zone(6) Open
Zone Resistance						50%	:	
Zone Support	50%	50%	43%	46%	43%	28%	:	
Zone Reached	6%	12%	22%	41%	72%	100%	:	
							:	Zone(5) Close, Zone(1) Open
Zone Resistance	67%	0%	50%	0%	100%		:	
Zone Support	17%						:	
Zone Reached	100%	33%	33%	17%	17%	0%	:	
							:	Zone(5) Close, Zone(2) Open
Zone Resistance		16%	81%	50%	0%	0%	:	
Zone Support	41%	32%					:	
Zone Reached	68%	100%	84%	24%	4%	4%	:	
							:	Zone(5) Close, Zone(3) Open
Zone Resistance			36%	73%	60%	50%	:	
Zone Support	50%	49%	29%				:	
Zone Reached	36%	71%	100%	67%	15%	6%	:	
							:	Zone(5) Close, Zone(4) Open
Zone Resistance				40%	54%	45%	:	
Zone Support	31%	69%	51%	34%			:	
Zone Reached	10%	32%	66%	100%	60%	28%	:	
							:	Zone(5) Close, Zone(5) Open
Zone Resistance					38%	43%	:	
Zone Support	25%	64%	35%	50%	29%		:	
Zone Reached	8%	23%	35%	71%	100%	62%	:	
							:	Zone(5) Close, Zone(6) Open
Zone Resistance						36%	:	
Zone Support	67%	0%	25%	43%	42%	14%	:	
Zone Reached	21%	21%	29%	50%	86%	100%	:	
							:	Zone(6) Close, Zone(1) Open
Zone Resistance	50%	100%					:	
Zone Support	25%						:	
Zone Reached	100%	50%	0%	0%	0%	0%	:	
							:	Zone(6) Close, Zone(2) Open
Zone Resistance		29%	47%	40%	20%	0%	:	
Zone Support	42%	50%					:	
Zone Reached	50%	100%	71%	42%	21%	17%	:	
							:	Zone(6) Close, Zone(3) Open
Zone Resistance			18%	70%	50%	29%	:	
Zone Support	45%	69%	37%				:	
Zone Reached	19%	63%	100%	82%	25%	12%	:	
							:	Zone(6) Close, Zone(4) Open
Zone Resistance				46%	64%	37%	:	
Zone Support	62%	70%	66%	41%			:	
Zone Reached	6%	20%	59%	100%	54%	19%	:	
							:	Zone(6) Close, Zone(5) Open
Zone Resistance					42%	55%	:	
Zone Support	0%	60%	55%	62%	24%		:	
Zone Reached	5%	13%	29%	76%	100%	58%	:	
							:	Zone(6) Close, Zone(6) Open
Zone Resistance						29%	:	
Zone Support	100%	50%	33%	25%	43%	59%	:	
Zone Reached	6%	12%	18%	24%	41%	100%	:	

ZONES (1) - (6) : ZONE(?) CLOSE, ZONE(?) OPEN

(1)	(2)	(3)	(4)	(5)	(6)		
						:	Zone(1) Close, Zone(1) Open
35%	18%	50%	29%	80%	100%	:	Zone Resistance
62%						:	Zone Support
100%	65%	54%	27%	19%	4%	:	Zone Reached
						:	Zone(1) Close, Zone(2) Open
	7%	72%	71%	50%	33%	:	Zone Resistance
47%	44%					:	Zone Support
56%	100%	93%	26%	7%	4%	:	Zone Reached
						:	Zone(1) Close, Zone(3) Open
		40%	56%	77%	50%	:	Zone Resistance
34%	72%	56%				:	Zone Support
12%	44%	100%	61%	26%	6%	:	Zone Reached
						:	Zone(1) Close, Zone(4) Open
			41%	63%	14%	:	Zone Resistance
0%	80%	77%	31%			:	Zone Support
3%	16%	69%	100%	59%	22%	:	Zone Reached
						:	Zone(1) Close, Zone(5) Open
				64%	0%	:	Zone Resistance
0%	0%	67%	40%	9%		:	Zone Support
18%	18%	55%	91%	100%	36%	:	Zone Reached
						:	Zone(1) Close, Zone(6) Open
					0%	:	Zone Resistance
					100%	:	Zone Support
0%	0%	0%	0%	0%	100%	:	Zone Reached
						:	Zone(2) Close, Zone(1) Open
28%	50%	67%	33%	0%	50%	:	Zone Resistance
32%						:	Zone Support
100%	72%	36%	12%	8%	8%	:	Zone Reached
						:	Zone(2) Close, Zone(2) Open
	4%	54%	46%	46%	57%	:	Zone Resistance
32%	48%					:	Zone Support
52%	100%	96%	44%	24%	13%	:	Zone Reached
						:	Zone(2) Close, Zone(3) Open
		27%	47%	62%	64%	:	Zone Resistance
49%	52%	52%				:	Zone Support
23%	48%	100%	73%	39%	15%	:	Zone Reached
						:	Zone(2) Close, Zone(4) Open
			40%	59%	31%	:	Zone Resistance
50%	69%	66%	28%			:	Zone Support
8%	25%	72%	100%	60%	25%	:	Zone Reached
						:	Zone(2) Close, Zone(5) Open
				33%	50%	:	Zone Resistance
0%	25%	20%	29%	42%		:	Zone Support
25%	33%	42%	58%	100%	67%	:	Zone Reached
						:	Zone(2) Close, Zone(6) Open
					20%	:	Zone Resistance
			100%	75%	20%	:	Zone Support
0%	0%	0%	20%	80%	100%	:	Zone Reached
						:	Zone(3) Close, Zone(1) Open
20%	62%	43%	25%	50%	33%	:	Zone Resistance
39%						:	Zone Support
100%	80%	30%	17%	13%	7%	:	Zone Reached
						:	Zone(3) Close, Zone(2) Open
	8%	45%	40%	42%	36%	:	Zone Resistance
33%	48%					:	Zone Support
52%	100%	92%	52%	30%	18%	:	Zone Reached
						:	Zone(3) Close, Zone(3) Open
		23%	50%	55%	39%	:	Zone Resistance
31%	60%	53%				:	Zone Support
19%	47%	100%	77%	39%	18%	:	Zone Reached
						:	Zone(3) Close, Zone(4) Open
			26%	51%	39%	:	Zone Resistance
29%	57%	63%	42%			:	Zone Support
9%	21%	58%	100%	74%	36%	:	Zone Reached
						:	Zone(3) Close, Zone(5) Open
				19%	44%	:	Zone Resistance
0%	33%	40%	74%	39%		:	Zone Support
6%	10%	16%	61%	100%	81%	:	Zone Reached
						:	Zone(3) Close, Zone(6) Open
					36%	:	Zone Resistance
0%	0%	0%	60%	44%	36%	:	Zone Support
14%	14%	14%	36%	64%	100%	:	Zone Reached

*** COFFEE ***

Z O N E S (1) - (6) : ZONE(?) CLOSE, ZONE(?) OPEN

(1)	(2)	(3)	(4)	(5)	(6)		
						:	**Zone(4) Close, Zone(1) Open**
12%	48%	50%	17%	20%	50%	:	Zone Resistance
46%						:	Zone Support
100%	88%	46%	23%	19%	15%	:	Zone Reached
						:	**Zone(4) Close, Zone(2) Open**
	9%	53%	52%	43%	25%	:	Zone Resistance
46%	46%					:	Zone Support
54%	100%	91%	43%	21%	12%	:	Zone Reached
						:	**Zone(4) Close, Zone(3) Open**
		20%	65%	61%	38%	:	Zone Resistance
33%	52%	45%				:	Zone Support
26%	55%	100%	80%	28%	11%	:	Zone Reached
						:	**Zone(4) Close, Zone(4) Open**
			32%	59%	43%	:	Zone Resistance
43%	59%	47%	37%			:	Zone Support
14%	33%	63%	100%	68%	28%	:	Zone Reached
						:	**Zone(4) Close, Zone(5) Open**
				30%	40%	:	Zone Resistance
33%	50%	37%	49%	26%		:	Zone Support
12%	24%	38%	74%	100%	70%	:	Zone Reached
						:	**Zone(4) Close, Zone(6) Open**
					59%	:	Zone Resistance
17%	0%	40%	33%	29%	28%	:	Zone Support
21%	21%	34%	52%	72%	100%	:	Zone Reached
						:	**Zone(5) Close, Zone(1) Open**
20%	75%	0%	0%	0%	0%	:	Zone Resistance
20%						:	Zone Support
100%	80%	20%	20%	20%	20%	:	Zone Reached
						:	**Zone(5) Close, Zone(2) Open**
	5%	37%	58%	20%	75%	:	Zone Resistance
60%	50%					:	Zone Support
50%	100%	95%	60%	25%	20%	:	Zone Reached
						:	**Zone(5) Close, Zone(3) Open**
		20%	73%	67%	17%	:	Zone Resistance
57%	70%	45%				:	Zone Support
17%	55%	100%	80%	22%	7%	:	Zone Reached
						:	**Zone(5) Close, Zone(4) Open**
			40%	60%	33%	:	Zone Resistance
40%	76%	63%	42%			:	Zone Support
5%	22%	58%	100%	60%	24%	:	Zone Reached
						:	**Zone(5) Close, Zone(5) Open**
				28%	55%	:	Zone Resistance
33%	25%	47%	52%	22%		:	Zone Support
15%	20%	38%	78%	100%	72%	:	Zone Reached
						:	**Zone(5) Close, Zone(6) Open**
					40%	:	Zone Resistance
	100%	0%	83%	14%	30%	:	Zone Support
0%	10%	10%	60%	70%	100%	:	Zone Reached
						:	**Zone(6) Close, Zone(1) Open**
29%	40%	67%	0%	0%	0%	:	Zone Resistance
57%						:	Zone Support
100%	71%	43%	14%	14%	14%	:	Zone Reached
						:	**Zone(6) Close, Zone(2) Open**
	14%	50%	33%	50%	100%	:	Zone Resistance
50%	71%					:	Zone Support
29%	100%	86%	43%	29%	14%	:	Zone Reached
						:	**Zone(6) Close, Zone(3) Open**
		20%	89%	100%		:	Zone Resistance
37%	50%	36%				:	Zone Support
32%	64%	100%	80%	8%	0%	:	Zone Reached
						:	**Zone(6) Close, Zone(4) Open**
			46%	61%	35%	:	Zone Resistance
50%	89%	63%	44%			:	Zone Support
2%	21%	56%	100%	54%	21%	:	Zone Reached
						:	**Zone(6) Close, Zone(5) Open**
				38%	32%	:	Zone Resistance
0%	25%	73%	52%	22%		:	Zone Support
8%	10%	38%	78%	100%	62%	:	Zone Reached
						:	**Zone(6) Close, Zone(6) Open**
					35%	:	Zone Resistance
67%	0%	0%	57%	46%	50%	:	Zone Support
12%	12%	12%	27%	50%	100%	:	Zone Reached

ZONES (1) - (6)   : ZONE(?) CLOSE, ZONE(?) OPEN

	(1)	(2)	(3)	(4)	(5)	(6)		
							:	Zone(1) Close, Zone(1) Open
Zone Resistance	39%	42%	73%	33%	50%	100%		
Zone Support	52%							
Zone Reached	100%	61%	35%	10%	6%	3%	:	
							:	Zone(1) Close, Zone(2) Open
Zone Resistance		25%	60%	38%	69%	25%		
Zone Support	34%	41%						
Zone Reached	59%	100%	75%	30%	19%	6%	:	
							:	Zone(1) Close, Zone(3) Open
Zone Resistance			36%	71%	68%	43%		
Zone Support	29%	67%	61%					
Zone Reached	13%	39%	100%	64%	18%	6%	:	
							:	Zone(1) Close, Zone(4) Open
Zone Resistance				48%	65%	33%		
Zone Support	50%	64%	74%	35%				
Zone Reached	6%	17%	65%	100%	52%	18%	:	
							:	Zone(1) Close, Zone(5) Open
Zone Resistance					69%	25%		
Zone Support	0%	80%	50%	17%	8%			
Zone Reached	8%	38%	77%	92%	100%	31%	:	
							:	Zone(1) Close, Zone(6) Open
Zone Resistance						67%	:	
Zone Support			100%	0%	33%	50%	:	
Zone Reached	0%	0%	33%	33%	50%	100%	:	
							:	Zone(2) Close, Zone(1) Open
Zone Resistance	42%	42%	64%	25%	0%	0%	:	
Zone Support	36%						:	
Zone Reached	100%	58%	33%	12%	9%	9%	:	
							:	Zone(2) Close, Zone(2) Open
Zone Resistance		12%	61%	50%	33%	33%	:	
Zone Support	57%	46%					:	
Zone Reached	54%	100%	88%	35%	17%	12%	:	
							:	Zone(2) Close, Zone(3) Open
Zone Resistance			30%	50%	64%	48%	:	
Zone Support	41%	61%	56%				:	
Zone Reached	17%	44%	100%	72%	35%	12%	:	
							:	Zone(2) Close, Zone(4) Open
Zone Resistance				23%	61%	42%	:	
Zone Support	33%	47%	67%	34%			:	
Zone Reached	11%	22%	66%	100%	77%	30%	:	
							:	Zone(2) Close, Zone(5) Open
Zone Resistance					35%	27%	:	
Zone Support		100%	75%	67%	48%		:	
Zone Reached	0%	4%	17%	52%	100%	65%	:	
							:	Zone(2) Close, Zone(6) Open
Zone Resistance						30%	:	
Zone Support	0%	0%	50%	0%	33%	70%	:	
Zone Reached	10%	10%	20%	20%	30%	100%	:	
							:	Zone(3) Close, Zone(1) Open
Zone Resistance	35%	56%	80%	67%	100%		:	
Zone Support	44%						:	
Zone Reached	100%	65%	29%	6%	2%	0%	:	
							:	Zone(3) Close, Zone(2) Open
Zone Resistance		21%	52%	52%	27%	27%	:	
Zone Support	44%	39%					:	
Zone Reached	61%	100%	79%	38%	18%	13%	:	
							:	Zone(3) Close, Zone(3) Open
Zone Resistance			24%	51%	63%	33%	:	
Zone Support	46%	54%	44%				:	
Zone Reached	26%	56%	100%	77%	36%	13%	:	
							:	Zone(3) Close, Zone(4) Open
Zone Resistance				24%	52%	41%	:	
Zone Support	25%	43%	61%	40%			:	
Zone Reached	13%	23%	60%	100%	76%	36%	:	
							:	Zone(3) Close, Zone(5) Open
Zone Resistance					35%	31%	:	
Zone Support	0%	50%	50%	60%	39%		:	
Zone Reached	6%	12%	24%	61%	100%	65%	:	
							:	Zone(3) Close, Zone(6) Open
Zone Resistance						33%	:	
Zone Support	0%	0%	50%	60%	55%	54%	:	
Zone Reached	4%	4%	8%	21%	46%	100%	:	

*** COCOA ***

Z O N E S (1) - (6)   : ZONE(?) CLOSE, ZONE(?) OPEN

Close / Open	Metric	(1)	(2)	(3)	(4)	(5)	(6)
Zone(4) Close, Zone(1) Open	Zone Resistance	29%	32%	53%	50%	0%	25%
	Zone Support	63%					
	Zone Reached	100%	71%	49%	23%	11%	11%
Zone(4) Close, Zone(2) Open	Zone Resistance		21%	44%	44%	32%	31%
	Zone Support	27%	43%				
	Zone Reached	57%	100%	79%	44%	25%	17%
Zone(4) Close, Zone(3) Open	Zone Resistance			29%	56%	60%	62%
	Zone Support	44%	56%	36%			
	Zone Reached	28%	64%	100%	71%	31%	13%
Zone(4) Close, Zone(4) Open	Zone Resistance				34%	56%	34%
	Zone Support	38%	60%	54%	35%		
	Zone Reached	12%	30%	65%	100%	66%	29%
Zone(4) Close, Zone(5) Open	Zone Resistance					29%	40%
	Zone Support	25%	67%	40%	57%	30%	
	Zone Reached	6%	18%	30%	70%	100%	71%
Zone(4) Close, Zone(6) Open	Zone Resistance						61%
	Zone Support	50%	0%	33%	50%	48%	36%
	Zone Reached	11%	11%	17%	33%	64%	100%
Zone(5) Close, Zone(1) Open	Zone Resistance	33%	50%	0%	33%	50%	100%
	Zone Support	33%					
	Zone Reached	100%	67%	33%	33%	22%	11%
Zone(5) Close, Zone(2) Open	Zone Resistance		20%	40%	50%	33%	50%
	Zone Support	54%	48%				
	Zone Reached	52%	100%	80%	48%	24%	16%
Zone(5) Close, Zone(3) Open	Zone Resistance			28%	65%	67%	0%
	Zone Support	47%	67%	31%			
	Zone Reached	23%	69%	100%	73%	24%	8%
Zone(5) Close, Zone(4) Open	Zone Resistance				43%	59%	34%
	Zone Support	35%	53%	51%	33%		
	Zone Reached	15%	33%	67%	100%	57%	23%
Zone(5) Close, Zone(5) Open	Zone Resistance					64%	17%
	Zone Support	0%	56%	44%	33%	27%	
	Zone Reached	12%	27%	48%	73%	100%	36%
Zone(5) Close, Zone(6) Open	Zone Resistance						27%
	Zone Support	0%	0%	0%	50%	71%	53%
	Zone Reached	7%	7%	7%	13%	47%	100%
Zone(6) Close, Zone(1) Open	Zone Resistance	57%	0%	33%	100%		
	Zone Support	71%					
	Zone Reached	100%	43%	43%	29%	0%	0%
Zone(6) Close, Zone(2) Open	Zone Resistance		18%	57%	40%	50%	100%
	Zone Support	58%	57%				
	Zone Reached	43%	100%	82%	36%	21%	11%
Zone(6) Close, Zone(3) Open	Zone Resistance			14%	62%	57%	58%
	Zone Support	54%	72%	45%			
	Zone Reached	15%	55%	100%	86%	33%	14%
Zone(6) Close, Zone(4) Open	Zone Resistance				52%	65%	44%
	Zone Support	60%	82%	52%	46%		
	Zone Reached	5%	26%	54%	100%	48%	17%
Zone(6) Close, Zone(5) Open	Zone Resistance					37%	47%
	Zone Support	50%	78%	25%	64%	33%	
	Zone Reached	4%	18%	24%	66%	98%	64%
Zone(6) Close, Zone(6) Open	Zone Resistance						60%
	Zone Support	33%	0%	0%	50%	40%	50%
	Zone Reached	15%	15%	15%	30%	50%	100%

ZONES (1) - (6)   : ZONE(?) CLOSE, ZONE(?) OPEN

(1)	(2)	(3)	(4)	(5)	(6)	:	
						:	Zone(1) Close, Zone(1) Open
42%	18%	56%	0%	50%	50%	:	Zone Resistance
53%						:	Zone Support
100%	58%	47%	21%	21%	11%	:	Zone Reached
						:	Zone(1) Close, Zone(2) Open
	3%	66%	25%	78%	50%	:	Zone Resistance
62%	33%					:	Zone Support
67%	100%	97%	33%	25%	6%	:	Zone Reached
						:	Zone(1) Close, Zone(3) Open
		39%	66%	77%	50%	:	Zone Resistance
61%	63%	57%				:	Zone Support
16%	43%	100%	62%	20%	5%	:	Zone Reached
						:	Zone(1) Close, Zone(4) Open
			21%	61%	33%	:	Zone Resistance
75%	64%	63%	23%			:	Zone Support
10%	28%	77%	100%	79%	31%	:	Zone Reached
						:	Zone(1) Close, Zone(5) Open
				75%	50%	:	Zone Resistance
100%	0%	75%	33%	25%		:	Zone Support
12%	12%	50%	75%	100%	25%	:	Zone Reached
						:	Zone(1) Close, Zone(6) Open
					25%	:	Zone Resistance
50%	33%	0%	0%	0%	25%	:	Zone Support
50%	75%	75%	75%	75%	100%	:	Zone Reached
						:	Zone(2) Close, Zone(1) Open
50%	25%	33%	0%	50%	100%	:	Zone Resistance
50%						:	Zone Support
100%	50%	38%	25%	25%	12%	:	Zone Reached
						:	Zone(2) Close, Zone(2) Open
	23%	56%	33%	25%	17%	:	Zone Resistance
23%	37%					:	Zone Support
63%	100%	77%	34%	23%	17%	:	Zone Reached
						:	Zone(2) Close, Zone(3) Open
		30%	57%	74%	43%	:	Zone Resistance
44%	62%	46%				:	Zone Support
21%	54%	100%	70%	30%	8%	:	Zone Reached
						:	Zone(2) Close, Zone(4) Open
			33%	72%	50%	:	Zone Resistance
40%	57%	62%	20%			:	Zone Support
13%	31%	80%	100%	67%	19%	:	Zone Reached
						:	Zone(2) Close, Zone(5) Open
				58%	60%	:	Zone Resistance
50%	0%	60%	50%	17%		:	Zone Support
17%	17%	42%	83%	100%	42%	:	Zone Reached
						:	Zone(2) Close, Zone(6) Open
					20%	:	Zone Resistance
				100%	80%	:	Zone Support
0%	0%	0%	0%	20%	100%	:	Zone Reached
						:	Zone(3) Close, Zone(1) Open
45%	42%	29%	20%	25%	0%	:	Zone Resistance
50%						:	Zone Support
100%	55%	32%	23%	18%	14%	:	Zone Reached
						:	Zone(3) Close, Zone(2) Open
	22%	58%	39%	18%	33%	:	Zone Resistance
45%	31%					:	Zone Support
69%	100%	78%	33%	20%	16%	:	Zone Reached
						:	Zone(3) Close, Zone(3) Open
		25%	54%	62%	35%	:	Zone Resistance
33%	59%	40%				:	Zone Support
25%	60%	100%	75%	34%	13%	:	Zone Reached
						:	Zone(3) Close, Zone(4) Open
			33%	55%	52%	:	Zone Resistance
50%	55%	53%	26%			:	Zone Support
16%	35%	74%	100%	67%	30%	:	Zone Reached
						:	Zone(3) Close, Zone(5) Open
				13%	38%	:	Zone Resistance
33%	25%	50%	64%	44%		:	Zone Support
8%	10%	21%	56%	100%	87%	:	Zone Reached
						:	Zone(3) Close, Zone(6) Open
					50%	:	Zone Resistance
			100%	60%	50%	:	Zone Support
0%	0%	0%	20%	50%	100%	:	Zone Reached

*** LIVE CATTLE ***

Z O N E S (1) - (6)   : ZONE(?) CLOSE, ZONE(?) OPEN

	(1)	(2)	(3)	(4)	(5)	(6)	
Zone(4) Close, Zone(1) Open							
Zone Resistance	32%	31%	22%	43%	50%	100%	
Zone Support	58%						
Zone Reached	100%	68%	47%	37%	21%	11%	
Zone(4) Close, Zone(2) Open							
Zone Resistance		33%	58%	60%	0%	75%	
Zone Support	36%	22%					
Zone Reached	78%	100%	67%	28%	11%	11%	
Zone(4) Close, Zone(3) Open							
Zone Resistance			30%	54%	58%	30%	
Zone Support	48%	58%	29%				
Zone Reached	30%	71%	100%	70%	32%	14%	
Zone(4) Close, Zone(4) Open							
Zone Resistance				37%	58%	27%	
Zone Support	55%	59%	51%	30%			
Zone Reached	14%	34%	70%	100%	63%	27%	
Zone(4) Close, Zone(5) Open							
Zone Resistance				27%		37%	
Zone Support	25%	33%	33%	57%	29%		
Zone Reached	14%	20%	31%	71%	100%	73%	
Zone(4) Close, Zone(6) Open							
Zone Resistance						38%	
Zone Support	0%	67%	40%	38%	11%	57%	
Zone Reached	5%	14%	24%	38%	43%	100%	
Zone(5) Close, Zone(1) Open							
Zone Resistance	29%	40%	33%	50%	100%		
Zone Support	71%						
Zone Reached	100%	71%	43%	29%	14%	0%	
Zone(5) Close, Zone(2) Open							
Zone Resistance		17%	40%	67%	0%	50%	
Zone Support	0%	58%					
Zone Reached	42%	100%	83%	50%	17%	17%	
Zone(5) Close, Zone(3) Open							
Zone Resistance			27%	70%	73%	50%	
Zone Support	27%	55%	31%				
Zone Reached	31%	69%	100%	75%	21%	6%	
Zone(5) Close, Zone(4) Open							
Zone Resistance				47%	60%	47%	
Zone Support	50%	67%	59%	36%			
Zone Reached	8%	26%	64%	100%	53%	21%	
Zone(5) Close, Zone(5) Open							
Zone Resistance					21%	47%	
Zone Support	0%	0%	80%	74%	21%		
Zone Reached	4%	4%	21%	79%	100%	79%	
Zone(5) Close, Zone(6) Open							
Zone Resistance						45%	
Zone Support	0%	0%	33%	0%	57%	36%	
Zone Reached	18%	18%	27%	27%	64%	100%	
Zone(6) Close, Zone(1) Open							
Zone Resistance	0%	0%	33%	0%	0%	50%	
Zone Support	33%						
Zone Reached	100%	100%	100%	67%	67%	67%	
Zone(6) Close, Zone(2) Open							
Zone Resistance		0%	17%	100%			
Zone Support	75%	33%					
Zone Reached	67%	100%	100%	83%	0%	0%	
Zone(6) Close, Zone(3) Open							
Zone Resistance			33%	58%	89%	100%	
Zone Support	44%	65%	28%				
Zone Reached	25%	72%	100%	72%	25%	3%	
Zone(6) Close, Zone(4) Open							
Zone Resistance				53%	61%	44%	
Zone Support	55%	74%	68%	50%			
Zone Reached	4%	16%	50%	100%	47%	19%	
Zone(6) Close, Zone(5) Open							
Zone Resistance					39%	35%	
Zone Support	100%	67%	40%	79%	14%		
Zone Reached	4%	11%	18%	86%	100%	61%	
Zone(6) Close, Zone(6) Open							
Zone Resistance						56%	
Zone Support	0%	67%	25%	33%	14%	56%	
Zone Reached	6%	19%	25%	38%	44%	100%	

*** LIVE HOGS ***

Z O N E S (1) - (6)   : ZONE(?) CLOSE, ZONE(?) OPEN

(1)	(2)	(3)	(4)	(5)	(6)		
						:	Zone(1) Close, Zone(1) Open
38%	27%	18%	56%	25%	33%	:	Zone Resistance
62%						:	Zone Support
100%	62%	46%	38%	17%	12%	:	Zone Reached
						:	Zone(1) Close, Zone(2) Open
	15%	48%	67%	75%	0%	:	Zone Resistance
44%	41%					:	Zone Support
59%	100%	85%	44%	15%	4%	:	Zone Reached
						:	Zone(1) Close, Zone(3) Open
		39%	63%	76%	50%	:	Zone Resistance
34%	65%	46%				:	Zone Support
19%	54%	100%	63%	22%	5%	:	Zone Reached
						:	Zone(1) Close, Zone(4) Open
			41%	62%	80%	:	Zone Resistance
	100%	85%	25%			:	Zone Support
0%	11%	75%	100%	59%	23%	:	Zone Reached
						:	Zone(1) Close, Zone(5) Open
				50%	0%	:	Zone Resistance
			100%	33%		:	Zone Support
0%	0%	0%	67%	100%	50%	:	Zone Reached
						:	Zone(1) Close, Zone(6) Open
					25%	:	Zone Resistance
			100%	50%	50%	:	Zone Support
0%	0%	0%	25%	50%	100%	:	Zone Reached
						:	Zone(2) Close, Zone(1) Open
29%	50%	33%	50%	0%	100%	:	Zone Resistance
47%						:	Zone Support
100%	71%	35%	24%	12%	12%	:	Zone Reached
						:	Zone(2) Close, Zone(2) Open
	13%	41%	44%	78%	100%	:	Zone Resistance
56%	48%					:	Zone Support
52%	100%	87%	52%	29%	6%	:	Zone Reached
						:	Zone(2) Close, Zone(3) Open
		30%	54%	68%	67%	:	Zone Resistance
48%	63%	43%				:	Zone Support
21%	57%	100%	70%	33%	11%	:	Zone Reached
						:	Zone(2) Close, Zone(4) Open
			19%	62%	40%	:	Zone Resistance
100%	88%	76%	47%			:	Zone Support
2%	12%	53%	100%	81%	31%	:	Zone Reached
						:	Zone(2) Close, Zone(5) Open
				22%	29%	:	Zone Resistance
	100%	50%	71%	22%		:	Zone Support
0%	11%	22%	78%	100%	78%	:	Zone Reached
						:	Zone(2) Close, Zone(6) Open
					0%	:	Zone Resistance
			100%	67%		:	Zone Support
0%	0%	0%	0%	33%	100%	:	Zone Reached
						:	Zone(3) Close, Zone(1) Open
50%	62%	0%	33%	50%	0%	:	Zone Resistance
44%						:	Zone Support
100%	50%	19%	19%	12%	6%	:	Zone Reached
						:	Zone(3) Close, Zone(2) Open
	25%	51%	55%	50%	40%	:	Zone Resistance
41%	35%					:	Zone Support
65%	100%	75%	37%	17%	8%	:	Zone Reached
						:	Zone(3) Close, Zone(3) Open
		27%	48%	61%	43%	:	Zone Resistance
29%	54%	39%				:	Zone Support
28%	61%	100%	74%	38%	15%	:	Zone Reached
						:	Zone(3) Close, Zone(4) Open
			29%	57%	49%	:	Zone Resistance
36%	66%	55%	31%			:	Zone Support
11%	31%	69%	100%	71%	31%	:	Zone Reached
						:	Zone(3) Close, Zone(5) Open
				34%	24%	:	Zone Resistance
0%	67%	62%	75%	27%		:	Zone Support
2%	7%	18%	73%	100%	66%	:	Zone Reached
						:	Zone(3) Close, Zone(6) Open
					40%	:	Zone Resistance
		100%	67%	50%	40%	:	Zone Support
0%	0%	10%	30%	60%	100%	:	Zone Reached

Z O N E S (1) - (6)   : ZONE(?) CLOSE, ZONE(?) OPEN

(1)	(2)	(3)	(4)	(5)	(6)	
						: Zone(4) Close, Zone(1) Open
38%	100%					: Zone Resistance
23%						: Zone Support
100%	62%	0%	0%	0%	0%	: Zone Reached
						: Zone(4) Close, Zone(2) Open
	21%	41%	40%	25%	44%	: Zone Resistance
59%	37%					: Zone Support
63%	100%	79%	47%	28%	21%	: Zone Reached
						: Zone(4) Close, Zone(3) Open
		28%	60%	59%	37%	: Zone Resistance
46%	50%	34%				: Zone Support
33%	66%	100%	73%	29%	12%	: Zone Reached
						: Zone(4) Close, Zone(4) Open
			38%	58%	40%	: Zone Resistance
47%	63%	51%	26%			: Zone Support
13%	37%	74%	100%	62%	26%	: Zone Reached
						: Zone(4) Close, Zone(5) Open
				25%	33%	: Zone Resistance
50%	50%	38%	64%	25%		: Zone Support
8%	17%	27%	75%	100%	75%	: Zone Reached
						: Zone(4) Close, Zone(6) Open
					35%	: Zone Resistance
		100%	75%	56%	47%	: Zone Support
0%	0%	6%	24%	53%	100%	: Zone Reached
						: Zone(5) Close, Zone(1) Open
0%	50%	0%	100%			: Zone Resistance
100%						: Zone Support
100%	100%	50%	50%	0%	0%	: Zone Reached
						: Zone(5) Close, Zone(2) Open
	14%	67%	50%	0%	100%	: Zone Resistance
67%	14%					: Zone Support
86%	100%	86%	29%	14%	14%	: Zone Reached
						: Zone(5) Close, Zone(3) Open
		21%	69%	71%	40%	: Zone Resistance
67%	67%	37%				: Zone Support
21%	63%	100%	81%	23%	7%	: Zone Reached
						: Zone(5) Close, Zone(4) Open
			49%	53%	50%	: Zone Resistance
42%	68%	58%	29%			: Zone Support
9%	30%	71%	100%	51%	24%	: Zone Reached
						: Zone(5) Close, Zone(5) Open
				32%	53%	: Zone Resistance
50%	67%	14%	61%	28%		: Zone Support
8%	24%	28%	72%	100%	68%	: Zone Reached
						: Zone(5) Close, Zone(6) Open
					30%	: Zone Resistance
	100%	50%	0%	50%	60%	: Zone Support
0%	10%	20%	20%	40%	100%	: Zone Reached
						: Zone(6) Close, Zone(1) Open
67%	0%	100%				: Zone Resistance
33%						: Zone Support
100%	33%	33%	0%	0%	0%	: Zone Reached
						: Zone(6) Close, Zone(2) Open
	17%	40%	67%	0%	0%	: Zone Resistance
67%	50%					: Zone Support
50%	100%	83%	50%	17%	17%	: Zone Reached
						: Zone(6) Close, Zone(3) Open
		31%	73%	78%	50%	: Zone Resistance
69%	63%	33%				: Zone Support
25%	67%	100%	71%	17%	4%	: Zone Reached
						: Zone(6) Close, Zone(4) Open
			50%	69%	46%	: Zone Resistance
43%	86%	65%	40%			: Zone Support
3%	21%	60%	100%	50%	15%	: Zone Reached
						: Zone(6) Close, Zone(5) Open
				25%	54%	: Zone Resistance
0%	33%	67%	61%	28%		: Zone Support
6%	9%	28%	72%	100%	75%	: Zone Reached
						: Zone(6) Close, Zone(6) Open
					50%	: Zone Resistance
50%	60%	17%	33%	18%	63%	: Zone Support
7%	17%	20%	30%	37%	100%	: Zone Reached

*** PORK BELLIES ***

Z O N E S (1) - (6)   : ZONE(?) CLOSE, ZONE(?) OPEN

(1)	(2)	(3)	(4)	(5)	(6)		
						:	Zone(1) Close, Zone(1) Open
48%	26%	25%	29%	33%	80%	:	Zone Resistance
38%						:	Zone Support
100%	52%	38%	29%	21%	14%	:	Zone Reached
						:	Zone(1) Close, Zone(2) Open
	16%	72%	40%	83%	100%	:	Zone Resistance
33%	23%					:	Zone Support
77%	100%	84%	23%	14%	2%	:	Zone Reached
						:	Zone(1) Close, Zone(3) Open
		38%	60%	85%	60%	:	Zone Resistance
54%	54%	42%				:	Zone Support
27%	58%	100%	63%	25%	4%	:	Zone Reached
						:	Zone(1) Close, Zone(4) Open
			42%	62%	50%	:	Zone Resistance
17%	40%	49%	13%			:	Zone Support
27%	44%	87%	100%	58%	22%	:	Zone Reached
						:	Zone(1) Close, Zone(5) Open
				58%	80%	:	Zone Resistance
33%	0%	62%	11%	25%		:	Zone Support
25%	25%	67%	75%	100%	42%	:	Zone Reached
						:	Zone(1) Close, Zone(6) Open
					0%	:	Zone Resistance
				100%	67%	:	Zone Support
0%	0%	0%	0%	33%	100%	:	Zone Reached
						:	Zone(2) Close, Zone(1) Open
35%	35%	36%	0%	29%	80%	:	Zone Resistance
42%						:	Zone Support
100%	65%	42%	27%	27%	19%	:	Zone Reached
						:	Zone(2) Close, Zone(2) Open
	24%	46%	53%	83%	100%	:	Zone Resistance
40%	26%					:	Zone Support
74%	100%	76%	44%	18%	3%	:	Zone Reached
						:	Zone(2) Close, Zone(3) Open
		26%	62%	69%	45%	:	Zone Resistance
31%	58%	47%				:	Zone Support
22%	53%	100%	74%	28%	9%	:	Zone Reached
						:	Zone(2) Close, Zone(4) Open
			30%	73%	25%	:	Zone Resistance
0%	75%	83%	24%			:	Zone Support
3%	13%	76%	100%	70%	19%	:	Zone Reached
						:	Zone(2) Close, Zone(5) Open
				62%	20%	:	Zone Resistance
67%	25%	20%	38%	38%		:	Zone Support
23%	31%	38%	62%	100%	38%	:	Zone Reached
						:	Zone(2) Close, Zone(6) Open
					17%	:	Zone Resistance
0%	0%	0%	0%	0%	83%	:	Zone Support
17%	17%	17%	17%	17%	100%	:	Zone Reached
						:	Zone(3) Close, Zone(1) Open
47%	67%	67%	100%			:	Zone Resistance
29%						:	Zone Support
100%	53%	18%	6%	0%	0%	:	Zone Reached
						:	Zone(3) Close, Zone(2) Open
	25%	48%	41%	20%	38%	:	Zone Resistance
30%	32%					:	Zone Support
68%	100%	75%	39%	23%	18%	:	Zone Reached
						:	Zone(3) Close, Zone(3) Open
		26%	49%	52%	46%	:	Zone Resistance
35%	55%	46%				:	Zone Support
24%	54%	100%	74%	38%	18%	:	Zone Reached
						:	Zone(3) Close, Zone(4) Open
			28%	57%	38%	:	Zone Resistance
52%	60%	66%	25%			:	Zone Support
10%	26%	75%	100%	72%	31%	:	Zone Reached
						:	Zone(3) Close, Zone(5) Open
				29%	41%	:	Zone Resistance
100%	67%	67%	55%	35%		:	Zone Support
3%	10%	29%	65%	100%	71%	:	Zone Reached
						:	Zone(3) Close, Zone(6) Open
					10%	:	Zone Resistance
	100%	0%	0%	83%	40%	:	Zone Support
0%	10%	10%	10%	60%	100%	:	Zone Reached

*** PORK BELLIES ***

Z O N E S (1) - (6)   : ZONE(?) CLOSE, ZONE(?) OPEN

(1)	(2)	(3)	(4)	(5)	(6)		
						:	Zone(4) Close, Zone(1) Open
60%	50%	100%				:	Zone Resistance
40%						:	Zone Support
100%	40%	20%	0%	0%	0%	:	Zone Reached
						:	Zone(4) Close, Zone(2) Open
	41%	63%	71%	0%	0%	:	Zone Resistance
21%	25%					:	Zone Support
75%	100%	59%	22%	6%	6%	:	Zone Reached
						:	Zone(4) Close, Zone(3) Open
		31%	50%	49%	49%	:	Zone Resistance
31%	44%	34%				:	Zone Support
37%	66%	100%	69%	34%	17%	:	Zone Reached
						:	Zone(4) Close, Zone(4) Open
			37%	48%	30%	:	Zone Resistance
39%	64%	52%	28%			:	Zone Support
13%	35%	72%	100%	63%	33%	:	Zone Reached
						:	Zone(4) Close, Zone(5) Open
				25%	37%	:	Zone Resistance
43%	53%	32%	46%	25%		:	Zone Support
13%	27%	40%	75%	100%	75%	:	Zone Reached
						:	Zone(4) Close, Zone(6) Open
					36%	:	Zone Resistance
0%	0%	75%	33%	33%	36%	:	Zone Support
7%	7%	29%	43%	64%	100%	:	Zone Reached
						:	Zone(5) Close, Zone(1) Open
50%	0%	100%				:	Zone Resistance
0%						:	Zone Support
100%	50%	50%	0%	0%	0%	:	Zone Reached
						:	Zone(5) Close, Zone(2) Open
	50%	67%	0%	100%		:	Zone Resistance
50%	33%					:	Zone Support
67%	100%	50%	17%	17%	0%	:	Zone Reached
						:	Zone(5) Close, Zone(3) Open
		22%	62%	35%	15%	:	Zone Resistance
60%	66%	34%				:	Zone Support
22%	66%	100%	78%	30%	19%	:	Zone Reached
						:	Zone(5) Close, Zone(4) Open
			55%	60%	29%	:	Zone Resistance
36%	64%	52%	29%			:	Zone Support
12%	34%	71%	100%	45%	18%	:	Zone Reached
						:	Zone(5) Close, Zone(5) Open
				30%	32%	:	Zone Resistance
100%	86%	36%	35%	37%		:	Zone Support
4%	26%	41%	63%	100%	70%	:	Zone Reached
						:	Zone(5) Close, Zone(6) Open
					28%	:	Zone Resistance
100%	50%	33%	25%	56%	50%	:	Zone Support
6%	11%	17%	22%	50%	100%	:	Zone Reached
						:	Zone(6) Close, Zone(1) Open
33%	17%	0%	0%	0%	60%	:	Zone Resistance
44%						:	Zone Support
100%	67%	56%	56%	56%	56%	:	Zone Reached
						:	Zone(6) Close, Zone(2) Open
	25%	56%	75%	100%		:	Zone Resistance
71%	42%					:	Zone Support
58%	100%	75%	33%	8%	0%	:	Zone Reached
						:	Zone(6) Close, Zone(3) Open
		20%	59%	54%	50%	:	Zone Resistance
50%	85%	35%				:	Zone Support
10%	65%	100%	80%	32%	15%	:	Zone Reached
						:	Zone(6) Close, Zone(4) Open
			48%	55%	38%	:	Zone Resistance
29%	81%	52%	35%			:	Zone Support
6%	31%	65%	100%	52%	23%	:	Zone Reached
						:	Zone(6) Close, Zone(5) Open
				16%	35%	:	Zone Resistance
	100%	71%	77%	16%		:	Zone Support
0%	5%	19%	84%	100%	84%	:	Zone Reached
						:	Zone(6) Close, Zone(6) Open
					34%	:	Zone Resistance
40%	29%	7%	32%	21%	57%	:	Zone Support
15%	22%	23%	34%	43%	100%	:	Zone Reached

```
          Z O N E S  (1) - (6)        : ZONE(?) CLOSE, ZONE(?) OPEN
```

(1)	(2)	(3)	(4)	(5)	(6)	
						: Zone(1) Close, Zone(1) Open
28%	43%	42%	29%	80%	0%	: Zone Resistance
48%						: Zone Support
100%	72%	41%	24%	17%	3%	: Zone Reached
						: Zone(1) Close, Zone(2) Open
	10%	74%	33%	43%	50%	: Zone Resistance
40%	48%					: Zone Support
52%	100%	90%	25%	15%	8%	: Zone Reached
						: Zone(1) Close, Zone(3) Open
		39%	59%	63%	33%	: Zone Resistance
34%	62%	63%				: Zone Support
14%	37%	100%	63%	23%	9%	: Zone Reached
						: Zone(1) Close, Zone(4) Open
			33%	64%	60%	: Zone Resistance
67%	40%	81%	38%			: Zone Support
7%	12%	62%	100%	67%	24%	: Zone Reached
						: Zone(1) Close, Zone(5) Open
				41%	50%	: Zone Resistance
50%	0%	71%	46%	24%		: Zone Support
12%	12%	41%	76%	100%	59%	: Zone Reached
						: Zone(1) Close, Zone(6) Open
					33%	: Zone Resistance
					100%	: Zone Support
0%	0%	0%	0%	0%	100%	: Zone Reached
						: Zone(2) Close, Zone(1) Open
38%	46%	57%	0%	33%	0%	: Zone Resistance
33%						: Zone Support
100%	62%	33%	14%	14%	10%	: Zone Reached
						: Zone(2) Close, Zone(2) Open
	7%	50%	56%	55%	20%	: Zone Resistance
44%	54%					: Zone Support
46%	100%	93%	46%	20%	9%	: Zone Reached
						: Zone(2) Close, Zone(3) Open
		37%	46%	75%	29%	: Zone Resistance
35%	71%	54%				: Zone Support
14%	46%	100%	65%	33%	8%	: Zone Reached
						: Zone(2) Close, Zone(4) Open
			26%	52%	37%	: Zone Resistance
0%	57%	79%	39%			: Zone Support
6%	13%	61%	100%	74%	35%	: Zone Reached
						: Zone(2) Close, Zone(5) Open
				18%	43%	: Zone Resistance
0%	50%	50%	27%	35%		: Zone Support
12%	24%	47%	65%	100%	82%	: Zone Reached
						: Zone(2) Close, Zone(6) Open
					100%	: Zone Resistance
		100%	0%	50%	0%	: Zone Support
0%	0%	50%	50%	100%	100%	: Zone Reached
						: Zone(3) Close, Zone(1) Open
23%	48%	33%	12%	43%	0%	: Zone Resistance
47%						: Zone Support
100%	77%	40%	27%	23%	13%	: Zone Reached
						: Zone(3) Close, Zone(2) Open
	23%	66%	44%	33%	25%	: Zone Resistance
23%	30%					: Zone Support
70%	100%	77%	28%	14%	9%	: Zone Reached
						: Zone(3) Close, Zone(3) Open
		26%	47%	59%	23%	: Zone Resistance
34%	57%	48%				: Zone Support
22%	52%	100%	77%	38%	15%	: Zone Reached
						: Zone(3) Close, Zone(4) Open
			29%	56%	48%	: Zone Resistance
10%	54%	54%	37%			: Zone Support
13%	29%	63%	100%	71%	31%	: Zone Reached
						: Zone(3) Close, Zone(5) Open
				29%	43%	: Zone Resistance
25%	33%	54%	52%	34%		: Zone Support
10%	14%	31%	64%	98%	71%	: Zone Reached
						: Zone(3) Close, Zone(6) Open
					35%	: Zone Resistance
0%	33%	25%	0%	60%	41%	: Zone Support
12%	18%	24%	24%	59%	100%	: Zone Reached

ZONES (1) - (6)   : ZONE(?) CLOSE, ZONE(?) OPEN

(1)	(2)	(3)	(4)	(5)	(6)		
						:	Zone(4) Close, Zone(1) Open
38%	62%	33%	50%	50%	100%	:	Zone Resistance
31%						:	Zone Support
100%	62%	23%	15%	8%	4%	:	Zone Reached
						:	Zone(4) Close, Zone(2) Open
	17%	57%	53%	44%	40%	:	Zone Resistance
35%	36%					:	Zone Support
64%	100%	83%	36%	17%	9%	:	Zone Reached
						:	Zone(4) Close, Zone(3) Open
		29%	57%	66%	29%	:	Zone Resistance
40%	54%	38%				:	Zone Support
29%	62%	100%	74%	29%	10%	:	Zone Reached
						:	Zone(4) Close, Zone(4) Open
			39%	55%	33%	:	Zone Resistance
36%	73%	62%	28%			:	Zone Support
7%	27%	72%	100%	61%	27%	:	Zone Reached
						:	Zone(4) Close, Zone(5) Open
				24%	51%	:	Zone Resistance
50%	78%	44%	48%	38%		:	Zone Support
4%	18%	31%	61%	98%	76%	:	Zone Reached
						:	Zone(4) Close, Zone(6) Open
					37%	:	Zone Resistance
0%	50%	0%	71%	30%	47%	:	Zone Support
5%	11%	11%	37%	53%	100%	:	Zone Reached
						:	Zone(5) Close, Zone(1) Open
20%	75%	50%	100%			:	Zone Resistance
20%						:	Zone Support
100%	80%	20%	10%	0%	0%	:	Zone Reached
						:	Zone(5) Close, Zone(2) Open
	24%	62%	60%	50%	0%	:	Zone Resistance
38%	24%					:	Zone Support
76%	100%	76%	29%	12%	6%	:	Zone Reached
						:	Zone(5) Close, Zone(3) Open
		8%	78%	45%	67%	:	Zone Resistance
33%	71%	33%				:	Zone Support
20%	67%	100%	95%	18%	10%	:	Zone Reached
						:	Zone(5) Close, Zone(4) .Open
			46%	62%	53%	:	Zone Resistance
47%	68%	55%	24%			:	Zone Support
11%	34%	75%	99%	54%	20%	:	Zone Reached
						:	Zone(5) Close, Zone(5) Open
				23%	35%	:	Zone Resistance
0%	75%	27%	63%	32%		:	Zone Support
5%	18%	25%	68%	100%	77%	:	Zone Reached
						:	Zone(5) Close, Zone(6) Open
					29%	:	Zone Resistance
			100%	75%	53%	:	Zone Support
0%	0%	0%	12%	47%	100%	:	Zone Reached
						:	Zone(6) Close, Zone(1) Open
25%	0%	67%	100%			:	Zone Resistance
75%						:	Zone Support
100%	75%	75%	25%	0%	0%	:	Zone Reached
						:	Zone(6) Close, Zone(2) Open
	7%	40%	67%	40%	33%	:	Zone Resistance
50%	70%					:	Zone Support
30%	100%	93%	56%	19%	11%	:	Zone Reached
						:	Zone(6) Close, Zone(3) Open
		27%	87%	25%	33%	:	Zone Resistance
36%	61%	29%				:	Zone Support
27%	71%	100%	75%	8%	6%	:	Zone Reached
						:	Zone(6) Close, Zone(4) Open
			54%	65%	34%	:	Zone Resistance
36%	74%	59%	38%			:	Zone Support
7%	25%	62%	100%	47%	17%	:	Zone Reached
						:	Zone(6) Close, Zone(5) Open
				31%	52%	:	Zone Resistance
0%	88%	47%	50%	29%		:	Zone Support
2%	19%	36%	71%	100%	69%	:	Zone Reached
						:	Zone(6) Close, Zone(6) Open
					47%	:	Zone Resistance
50%	0%	0%	67%	40%	41%	:	Zone Support
12%	12%	12%	35%	59%	100%	:	Zone Reached

Z O N E S (1) - (6)   : ZONE(?) CLOSE, ZONE(?) OPEN

(1)	(2)	(3)	(4)	(5)	(6)		
						:	Zone(1) Close, Zone(1) Open
37%	41%	60%	0%	25%	67%	:	Zone Resistance
52%						:	Zone Support
100%	63%	37%	15%	15%	11%	:	Zone Reached
						:	Zone(1) Close, Zone(2) Open
	18%	81%	50%	100%		:	Zone Resistance
29%	37%					:	Zone Support
63%	100%	82%	16%	8%	0%	:	Zone Reached
						:	Zone(1) Close, Zone(3) Open
		39%	68%	69%	33%	:	Zone Resistance
47%	64%	44%				:	Zone Support
20%	56%	100%	61%	20%	6%	:	Zone Reached
						:	Zone(1) Close, Zone(4) Open
			50%	58%	36%	:	Zone Resistance
50%	60%	74%	25%			:	Zone Support
8%	19%	75%	100%	50%	21%	:	Zone Reached
						:	Zone(1) Close, Zone(5) Open
				55%	40%	:	Zone Resistance
100%	0%	60%	29%	36%		:	Zone Support
18%	18%	45%	64%	100%	45%	:	Zone Reached
						:	Zone(1) Close, Zone(6) Open
					100%	:	Zone Resistance
0%	0%	50%	0%	33%	25%	:	Zone Support
25%	25%	50%	50%	75%	100%	:	Zone Reached
						:	Zone(2) Close, Zone(1) Open
40%	33%	83%	0%	0%	100%	:	Zone Resistance
20%						:	Zone Support
100%	60%	40%	13%	7%	7%	:	Zone Reached
						:	Zone(2) Close, Zone(2) Open
	20%	61%	62%	20%	25%	:	Zone Resistance
22%	34%					:	Zone Support
66%	100%	80%	32%	12%	10%	:	Zone Reached
						:	Zone(2) Close, Zone(3) Open
		27%	51%	65%	46%	:	Zone Resistance
41%	64%	51%				:	Zone Support
18%	49%	100%	73%	35%	12%	:	Zone Reached
						:	Zone(2) Close, Zone(4) Open
			30%	60%	39%	:	Zone Resistance
33%	67%	79%	34%			:	Zone Support
5%	14%	66%	100%	70%	28%	:	Zone Reached
						:	Zone(2) Close, Zone(5) Open
				36%	14%	:	Zone Resistance
100%	50%	50%	33%	45%		:	Zone Support
9%	18%	36%	55%	100%	64%	:	Zone Reached
						:	Zone(2) Close, Zone(6) Open
					0%	:	Zone Resistance
			100%	50%	0%	:	Zone Support
0%	0%	0%	50%	100%	100%	:	Zone Reached
						:	Zone(3) Close, Zone(1) Open
30%	63%	57%	25%	50%	0%	:	Zone Resistance
33%						:	Zone Support
100%	70%	26%	15%	7%	4%	:	Zone Reached
						:	Zone(3) Close, Zone(2) Open
	12%	36%	47%	61%	67%	:	Zone Resistance
40%	47%					:	Zone Support
53%	100%	88%	57%	30%	12%	:	Zone Reached
						:	Zone(3) Close, Zone(3) Open
		26%	55%	64%	41%	:	Zone Resistance
39%	52%	45%				:	Zone Support
26%	55%	100%	74%	33%	12%	:	Zone Reached
						:	Zone(3) Close, Zone(4) Open
			34%	50%	36%	:	Zone Resistance
46%	55%	61%	38%			:	Zone Support
11%	24%	62%	100%	66%	33%	:	Zone Reached
						:	Zone(3) Close, Zone(5) Open
				35%	64%	:	Zone Resistance
50%	78%	59%	39%	16%		:	Zone Support
5%	21%	51%	84%	100%	65%	:	Zone Reached
						:	Zone(3) Close, Zone(6) Open
					29%	:	Zone Resistance
0%	50%	0%	33%	57%	50%	:	Zone Support
7%	14%	14%	21%	50%	100%	:	Zone Reached

*** COTTON ***

Z O N E S (1) - (6) : ZONE(?) CLOSE, ZONE(?) OPEN

(1)	(2)	(3)	(4)	(5)	(6)		
						:	Zone(4) Close, Zone(1) Open
41%	31%	44%	80%	0%	0%	:	Zone Resistance
41%						:	Zone Support
100%	59%	41%	23%	5%	5%	:	Zone Reached
						:	Zone(4) Close, Zone(2) Open
	25%	49%	38%	58%	20%	:	Zone Resistance
34%	44%					:	Zone Support
56%	100%	75%	40%	23%	10%	:	Zone Reached
						:	Zone(4) Close, Zone(3) Open
		27%	59%	45%	38%	:	Zone Resistance
37%	62%	36%				:	Zone Support
24%	64%	100%	74%	30%	16%	:	Zone Reached
						:	Zone(4) Close, Zone(4) Open
			45%	54%	38%	:	Zone Resistance
36%	55%	52%	30%			:	Zone Support
15%	33%	69%	100%	55%	25%	:	Zone Reached
						:	Zone(4) Close, Zone(5) Open
				25%	37%	:	Zone Resistance
50%	40%	38%	43%	30%		:	Zone Support
15%	25%	40%	70%	100%	75%	:	Zone Reached
						:	Zone(4) Close, Zone(6) Open
					46%	:	Zone Resistance
0%	33%	40%	55%	31%	33%	:	Zone Support
8%	12%	21%	46%	67%	100%	:	Zone Reached
						:	Zone(5) Close, Zone(1) Open
33%	50%	0%	0%	0%	100%	:	Zone Resistance
33%						:	Zone Support
100%	67%	33%	33%	33%	33%	:	Zone Reached
						:	Zone(5) Close, Zone(2) Open
	21%	33%	40%	100%		:	Zone Resistance
22%	53%					:	Zone Support
47%	100%	79%	53%	32%	0%	:	Zone Reached
						:	Zone(5) Close, Zone(3) Open
		17%	67%	53%	43%	:	Zone Resistance
36%	69%	33%				:	Zone Support
20%	67%	100%	83%	28%	13%	:	Zone Reached
						:	Zone(5) Close, Zone(4) Open
			45%	48%	45%	:	Zone Resistance
60%	73%	58%	31%			:	Zone Support
8%	29%	69%	100%	55%	29%	:	Zone Reached
						:	Zone(5) Close, Zone(5) Open
				31%	24%	:	Zone Resistance
67%	62%	47%	52%	26%		:	Zone Support
7%	19%	36%	74%	100%	69%	:	Zone Reached
						:	Zone(5) Close, Zone(6) Open
					16%	:	Zone Resistance
100%	0%	0%	0%	88%	58%	:	Zone Support
5%	5%	5%	5%	42%	100%	:	Zone Reached
						:	Zone(6) Close, Zone(1) Open
29%	60%	0%	0%	0%	100%	:	Zone Resistance
14%						:	Zone Support
100%	71%	29%	29%	29%	29%	:	Zone Reached
						:	Zone(6) Close, Zone(2) Open
	21%	64%	20%	33%	50%	:	Zone Resistance
33%	36%					:	Zone Support
64%	100%	79%	36%	21%	14%	:	Zone Reached
						:	Zone(6) Close, Zone(3) Open
		24%	69%	44%	67%	:	Zone Resistance
50%	75%	44%				:	Zone Support
14%	56%	100%	77%	23%	13%	:	Zone Reached
						:	Zone(6) Close, Zone(4) Open
			51%	59%	30%	:	Zone Resistance
47%	73%	63%	45%			:	Zone Support
6%	21%	55%	100%	49%	20%	:	Zone Reached
						:	Zone(6) Close, Zone(5) Open
				38%	25%	:	Zone Resistance
0%	60%	50%	52%	19%		:	Zone Support
8%	19%	38%	81%	100%	62%	:	Zone Reached
						:	Zone(6) Close, Zone(6) Open
					50%	:	Zone Resistance
80%	0%	17%	25%	27%	54%	:	Zone Support
21%	21%	25%	33%	46%	100%	:	Zone Reached